A Memoir

My Life, Loves, and Laughs

For Lillian Daniel,
With Thanks
for your ministry

Garrett Ward Sheldon

A Memoir
My Life, Loves, and Laughs

ISBN: 978-0-9966890-6-9

Soft Cover

HopeWay Publishers
Gate City, Virginia 24251
HopeWayBooks.com
hopewaybooks@gmail.com

Dedication

Tim Dotson, Sam Henry, Phil Henry

Who built the loft where this book was written. . .

"For in your hidden providence Your hands, my God did not forsake my soul... 'For the steps of man are directed by the Lord, and he chooses his way."   *(Psalms 36.23)*

"...in this also your profoundly mysterious providence and your mercy very present to us are proper matters for reflection and proclamation."   *St. Augustine*
                                               Confessions

Table of Contents

Preface

In my 66th year, I am writing memories of a life from 1954 to the present. It is to detail an interesting and blessed life during an era in America that is rapidly disappearing. So, it is primarily for family and friends interested in my life and for future generations interested in the society, culture, and manners of a middle-class existence in mid-20th Century America. An added, and perhaps more immediate benefit, is the opportunity for self-reflection and understanding. Everyone should write an autobiography, or at least keep a diary or journal, because, in putting down the thoughts and events of one's life, one sees and understands them more. As St. Augustine said, "Our reflections will be multiplied at His prompting. Thus, in our service of Him we will suffer no shortage but will rather rejoice in a miraculous abundance of ideas."

In preparing for this Memoir, I read many autobiographies of favorite writers and personalities: the American Founder, Thomas Jefferson; my Great grandfather, Charles M. Sheldon, author of *In His Steps*; the popular 20th Century Christian writer, C. S. Lewis; and the English essayists and humorists P.G. Wodehouse; Evelyn Waugh; Sir John Mortimer; Osbert Lancaster; and Kingsley Amis.

Those familiar with these Edwardian characters will know that my affinity for them explains a lot about my character and background. The greatest Christian memoir is St. Augustine's Confessions, and it is a model for seeing one's life as led by and infused with God's grace and providence. The two greatest things I think we can leave this sad world are our Faith and a laugh: Truth, Comfort, and Cheering-up. If any readers of this book receive that, it will be a success and I will be very grateful.

Garrett Ward Sheldon
Powell Valley, Virginia
August 20, 2020

Ancestry

Thomas Jefferson, in his autobiography, described the two branches of his ancestry as very different. His father came from humble Welsh stock, and had little formal education, but distinguished himself as an expert Surveyor of the Virginia Colony, receiving as a reward from the Crown, several thousand acres.

Jefferson's aristocratic mother's family, the Randolphs, he wrote, "trace their pedigree far back in England and Scotland, to which let everyone ascribe the faith and merit he chooses."

My family ancestry is similarly different, though in reverse: my mother's (Garrett) family was humble and obscure, while my father's lineage contained many illustrious personages.

Little is known of my mother's ancestry. Her father, Frederick Garrett, I never knew, as he died before I was born (but photographs show a striking resemblance). He owned a photographic studio in Green Bay, Wisconsin, having served as an aerial photographer in World War I. Whenever I asked my grandma about him, she only sighed and said in a sort of apologetic way, "he was a *good man*", suggesting to me that she found him rather boring.

His father was a circuit-riding Methodist preacher during the Second Great Awakening revival of the mid-1800s. His sister, our Aunt Flora, was a maiden lady of the most severe Victorian type who served as a librarian in Oshkosh, Wisconsin. My Grandma Garrett's father, by the German name "Raidler", was an engineer on a railroad. His wife's maiden name was "Davis" from the South, but I know nothing of that possibly illustrious lineage.

My father's family of Sheldon, Ward, Merriam, Kelloge, Hopkins, and Harmen trace their ancestry far back in English and Irish history with many distinguished "teachers and preachers". Including Gilbert Sheldon, Archbishop of Canterbury in the late 1600s under the Restoration King Charles II, who built the Sheldonian Theatre (auditorium) at Oxford University for which my family was always proud. One summer evening in Oxford, I was outside the Sheldonian looking at the concert poster when a young English lady carrying a violin case came up to me and said, "Excuse me, but do you have any connection with the Sheldonian?"

I swelled with pride and replied, "Why YES!"

She said, "Well do you have a key? I can't get in." Apparently, she mistook me for the janitor or custodian...

Other notable figures from my father's side of the family included Anglo-Irish, English, and American clergy, including the Episcopal Bishop who wrote the Christian Hymn *"We Three Kings"*. Also, my Great-grandfather Charles M. Sheldon, a Congregational Minister, wrote the famous Christian novel, *In His Steps* which (partly due to a faulty copyright) has been translated into twenty languages and sold an estimated thirty million copies, making it the most popular Christian book after the Bible.

Other relations of that branch of the family included lawyers, judges, bankers, businessmen, and academics. Solid, upper-middle-class, "old-money" professional people. Not rich, but solid, conservative "bourgeois" respectable leaders of their professions and communities, emphasizing hard work, education, saving money, and passing on an estate to their children – respectable and predictable. At least on the surface. But beneath, a large quota of eccentric, insane, alcoholic, high-strung, suicidal, and artistic types.

My original American ancestor was Isaac Sheldon, an English Puritan who settled in Massachusetts in the 1640s. His story is very mysterious. He came over to New England at the time of the English Civil War with his two brothers (all young) accompanied by a clergyman, not his parents. One wonders if something had happened to his parents during that tumultuous 17th Century in England or perhaps, they sent their boys away to avoid being drawn into the conflict.

I once visited the Midlands (North-central) of England (Derbyshire, near Bakewell) where his family resided for hundreds of years. I even visited the tiny village of "Sheldon" (though the tour guide said, "You don't want to go THERE!" presumably because it consisted of a church, a pub, and a few houses in the middle of nowhere. Also, the ancestral home around the Wye Valley bore a striking resemblance to my current home in the mountains of Southwest Virginia: tall mountains, broad valleys, and bright sky. It is no wonder I felt "at home" here the moment I arrived almost 40 years ago.

That early American ancestor, Issac Sheldon, owned most of the Connecticut Valley, but producing 18 children from three successive wives, the property was soon dispersed. One of the family houses in Northampton, Massachusetts was actually transported intact by canal barge to Princeton, New Jersey, where today it is still known as the Sheldon House. I have a copy of his will which included leaving a "wagonload of wheat for the "Scholars of Harvard College"". I mentioned that when I visited Harvard, but they were unimpressed – I didn't even get a free lunch out of it!

Another illustrious New England ancestor was Artemis Ward, Commander of the American Revolutionary Army before General George Washington was appointed. Ward, head of the Massachusetts Militia, was widely regarded as incompetent to lead the Continental Army.

Like most early Northeasterners, my family gradually migrated west to Vermont, Upstate New York, New Hampshire, and on to the Middle West (Michigan, Wisconsin, Kansas).

My current family did the DNA Ancestry test and it predictably showed my English, Irish, and German backgrounds, but also offered a surprising lineage: "West Asian". That apparently runs from Turkey to the Iberian Peninsula and on to the Middle East. Perhaps Sir Keith Sheldon brought back some souvenirs from the Third Crusade...But it does not explain why when I was in Istanbul, I was regularly mistaken for a Turk!

Family ancestry is interesting, but I'm not sure how much it tells us about a person. An individual is made of so many influences, biological, cultural, social, and psychological. God's divine plan for the individual. Although there is a distinct *physical* resemblance among many of my family members, each has such a distinct personality that it is difficult to see how much is hereditary.

My beloved NaNa as an infant; my great-grandparents, the Kelloggs, and My great-great grandmother Adams

CHILDHOOD

It is a blessing to me that in his memoir, *Surprised by Joy*, my favorite Christian writer, C. S. Lewis, described a childhood home almost as dysfunctional as my own. There is comfort in knowing that others, especially those we admire, have experienced some of the suffering we have suffered.

Like my parents, Lewis's mother was a kind, gentle, intelligent Christian woman who died young. His father, like mine, was emotionally unstable, filled with anger and hatred, and emotionally abusive.

I suppose today my father would be called a "Narcissistic Personality" — totally absorbed with himself, selfish, and demanding all the attention and praise. The most "self-centered" person I've ever known.

He was envious to the point of hatred of anyone who had anything or was anything he was not, even his own children. I recall one summer vacation from school, when
I was about ten, he came home from work and yelled at me because I got to stay home while he had to go out to work.

His bad temper was almost constant: angry and yelling, critical and sarcastic; he seemed to hate everyone. My mother once told my grandmother that, when he came home from work, we young children would "scatter like mice", running and hiding in fear of his wrath.

Again, today, I think psychologists would say he was a Sociopath – unable to have healthy human relationships. He had to dominate and control everyone and everything around him. To do this he employed many methods: from flattering and generosity to threats and terror. Like a psychopath, if he could not totally control and use others for his own purposes, he would have to destroy them, as he did my mother: driving her to alcoholism and eventually suicide.

The only creature that was wholly subservient to him was our dog, a sweet, loving dachshund, who was totally devoted to him. But even she was subject to his temper if she dared to sniff a piece of food that he offered her, taking it as an insult and yelling, "Eat that! It's good! I wouldn't give you anything bad!!!" Frightening.

In theological terms, my father displayed the "Original Sin" detailed in the Book of Genesis, as wanting and expecting to be God and have everything in the universe obey him and everyone worship him. In the Judeo-Christian view, everyone is tainted with this sin of pride, but most of us don't openly display it constantly. But he did, as though he deserved to have all power.

His behavior drove away all his family and friends. Once again at our cottage, my wife held our 6-month-old baby son and comforted his crying and my father yelled, "Don't pay attention to HIM! Pay attention to ME!" A more thoroughly selfish, hateful person I have ever known.

His personality was so extreme that I believe it had a physiological source. He was born six weeks premature in 1925, when most such babies died immediately and those who lived were put in incubators to be kept warm and fed. The isolation from human contact, I think, may have scarred him for life and he never could socialize with others. We now know the vital importance of giving the newborn baby to its mother right away, as even the first moments of life affect the child's mental and emotional development.

But, whatever the reason, my father made our family life a living hell. My siblings and I were brought up by the church to "Honor Thy Father and Mother", so we put up with his tirades and, even after we were grown and moved away, we kept in contact with him, albeit at a distance, and sent him cards and gifts, called regularly, and showed him respect.

Perhaps that Christian forbearance and duty led to the privilege of leading him to Christ in his 69th year. I had returned home from church one Sunday to find a telephone message from him, asking me to call him. When I did, he, obviously crying, said, "I just wanted to say, 'I love you'," Surprised by his words and tone, I replied, "Well, I love you, too Dad; and Christ loves you." He came to faith that afternoon of the day, and he later told me, he was going to kill himself that night. His second wife had finally had enough and left him in no uncertain terms and he finally confronted the evil in his character and life. (The classic Christian conversion.)

He clearly was "a new creature in Christ": humble and kind. I encouraged him to find a loving church and he grew in the Lord. But, as with most older converts, it is easy for the "old man" (as St Paul puts it) to "come back out" and in time, mental and physical infirmities led to his prior conduct to show itself more frequently. But he was contrite in a way he'd never been before his conversion.

He also was diagnosed as bipolar or "manic-depressive" having wild swings between excitement/hyperactivity (manic) and deep gloom and passivity (depressive). He had apparently had this for years before the condition was widely known and with many others with the condition (self-medicated" – drinking some three to four posts of coffee a day (caffeine to overcome depression) and drinking large amounts of liquor (whiskey) at night (to address manic hyperactivity).

When drugs came out to treat bipolar disorder, he refused to take them because he would have to give up drinking. He died at age 84 and I believe is in Heaven with his Savior Jesus, reunited with my mother in a loving union, and when I see him again, he will be a healthy, joyful, good person God intended him to be for eternity!

And the torture he made my childhood, like C.S. Lewis's, was mitigated by two things: other wonderful family members and the family dog. The main family salvation was my maternal grandmother or "NaNa", Cordelia Kellogg Sheldon. I will devote a large section of the memoir to this extraordinary persona, who provided stability, love, hospitality, generosity, fun, caring, and happiness amid this domestic turmoil. She didn't live with us, but her gorgeous, welcoming home was nearby in Whitefish Bay, Wisconsin, and my brother, sister and I were frequent visitors to this haven of peace, happiness, and normality. I hate to think of what may have become of us without this calming, secure, loving presence. We had every excuse, given our domestic abuse, to get into drugs and crime, ending up in prison, a mental institution, or the graveyard.

The family dog, a female dachshund (runt of the litter) "Sissy" was just a constant source of love and affection, always cheerful, fun, loving, and happy – a light in a dark place that made all the difference. The role of family pets in mental and domestic health cannot be underestimated. I honestly think, sometimes, that God sent our family an angel in the form of a dog.

Also, my siblings. My sister Barbara was five years older and a bit aloof from her goofy younger brother. She was very intellectual and stayed sequestered in her room reading or playing her guitar and singing. She graduated first in her high school class and gave the Valedictorian speech. Despite this seriousness, she had a sly sense of humor and a delightful laugh.

My brother Chuck was four years older and like many younger brothers, I revered him. He was strong, weight-lifting, athletic, could fix or make anything, and by about age fourteen had long sideburns! A real man. Cool. Despite his frequent teasing, Chuck taught me the tougher side of life and we have remained close all our lives.

The other saving grace in my childhood was to grow up in a very stable social culture, in the middle class of the Upper Midwest of America (Wisconsin) in the 1950s. If you've ever seen the television "Leave it to Beaver" show you know what I mean.

A social culture of morality; a strong work ethic, education, respect, responsibility, and orderliness permeated that place and era, reinforced by family (at least outwardly), school, church, community, media, law, and government. This placed definite limits on acceptable behavior. Politeness and a sense of responsibility undergirded that society, preserving a safe, orderly (if somewhat boring) environment.

We've joked that Midwestern culture added several commandments to the Biblical Ten Commandments.

Commandment 11
Thou Shalt Be Polite – Always

Commandment 12
Thou Shalt Be Discreet

Commandment 13
Thou Shalt Not Be Nosey

Commandment 14
Thou Shalt Mind Thy Own Business

Commandment 15
Thou Shalt Never Be Rude, Self-Assertive,
Profane or Obscene

Commandment 16
Thou Shalt Always Assume the Best about Others and
Never Condemn without Overwhelming Evidence

Another television series that exhibited this ethic was The *Bob Newhart Show* of the 1970's in which he plays a psychologist in Chicago. His reserve and politeness, even in the midst of extreme behavior display it. This Midwest reserve may explain why moving to the South was, at first, a challenge...

Again, since the turmoil in my home, I don't know what may have happened if it had occurred in the society of today, with its lack of standards, chaos, and lack of commitment. I'm afraid I would not have managed as well as I did.

This changed in my teens (the late 1960's –early 1970's) for me and American society, but my early social environment was very stable, orderly, and predictable. The East Side of Milwaukee, Wisconsin of my youth in the 1950s was often said to be "Not so much a city as a 'large German village'. "Safe, solid, secure, orderly. It was clean and beautiful with large green parks bordering Lake Michigan with European Gothic or Baroque architecture downtown, wide boulevards, and grand Victorian houses.

The Sheldon Home

It was such a safe, orderly community that my friends and I rode our bikes all over our neighborhood, at all times of the day and night, without fear. Few people even locked their doors in their houses. Honesty and self-control ruled the character of those people.

I recall riding my bike from our house on the east side of Milwaukee about six blocks over to the nearest shopping district on Downer Avenue. There (probably at the age of seven) I discovered a small bookshop owned by a kindly elderly lady. I would browse among the books for hours, and probably on her advice, acquired the early *Peanuts* comics and youthful detective stories *The Hardy Boys.*

Such a sheltered social environment, despite our domestic woes, led to a kind of naivete, even innocence. We knew nothing of crime or poverty, drugs or violence. Real evil was hidden from us. The Hardy Boys adventure books I read as a child show that Midwest middle-class innocence.

Also, Evelyn Waugh's autobiography, *A Little Learning,* reveals the culture in Edwardian England he grew up in. It was a culture of both Victorian morality and 19th-century romanticism and sentimentality. Both informed a "Gentleman's Code" of manners, honor, and loyalty. Bertie Wooster in the P.G.

Wodehouse Jeeves' stories humorously reveal it. Certain attitudes towards family, money, and women prevailed. For example, we were never to talk about money (one's income, what things cost, etc.) as that was considered "commercial" and vulgar or "common". Of course, always having enough money made that easier. Poorer people have to think about money.

But like Aristotle's definition of the "Good Life", money exists to free one to "higher" things (intellectual, artistic, spiritual) and so, to continue to be concerned about material things after one had "enough" was a kind of slavery. The Puritan heritage of having a good, solid house (comfortable but not ostentatious); solid (if plain) food: and sturdy (if plain) clothes influenced this attitude. But a grand "gaudy" house or fancy food or flashy clothes was looked down upon — they were signs of "new money", superficiality, and poor taste.

The attitude towards women came both from Medieval chivalry and 18th and 19th Century Romanticism. All women were considered virtuous. Women are naturally kind, gentle, unselfish, loving, and caring holders of morality. Men are selfish brutes, aggressive, and thoughtless. Women are made by God to civilize men through love, marriage, family, and religion.

I grew up believing that. It didn't help that my teachers, churchwomen, mother, sister, and NaNa were all saintly paragons of feminine virtue. I never met a crude, profane, aggressive, violent female. Women were to civilize the world through marriage and motherhood, while men slugged it out in business and politics. Women were superior in intellect, sensitivity, and morality. Feminists later rejected this "being put on a pedestal" and wanted to be denied as "sex objects" with beautiful hair and clothes and treated the same as men.

I was so naive about this that in my late 20s, at an academic conference, I met a man who introduced himself as "the Chaplain of the Women's Prison in Kansas". I thought he was kidding. There couldn't be a "Women's Prison" because a woman wouldn't commit a crime! When I told that story to a local butcher, he said, "You obviously haven't been to some of the bars I've been to! Some women are fiercer fighters than any man!" I have since learned that he was right...

Another cultural standard in the era I grew up in was the Biblical injunction to only have sex after marriage, against both fornication (sex before marriage) and adultery (sex outside of marriage). As the old Catholic school teaching went: "Sex is for procreation, not recreation".

In the 1950s middle America, before the "new Morality" of casual sex in the 1960s that has done such damage to marriage and family that Biblical standard was reinforced to young men by this threat: if you have sex with a girl, she may become pregnant. You will then have to marry her, leave school, and spend the rest of your life at a menial job (in a factory or gas station) supporting your family. This was before birth control, legal abortion, and easy divorce laws. The emotional and social damage of this promiscuity has plagued our nation ever since the mid-1960s"s. Not that everyone was pure and chaste before that (they surely were not) but the social standard kept things pretty orderly with stable, if not always happy, marriages and families; respecting fatherhood, honoring motherhood and responsibility.

As I often told my students when we covered the conservative philosopher Edmund Burke, when I grew up, I didn't think you could do anything else. Everyone went to school, got a job, got married, had children, worked hard, sacrificed, and that lifestyle ultimately produced greater happiness than staying single, casual transient relationships, and spending all one's money on oneself. It's probably best that I didn't know there were options...

In your 20's it's hard to imagine work, discipline, and sacrifice as preferable to absolute freedom, selfishness, and independence. But by your 40s you realize it was best to "put your nose to the grindstone", work and gain respect, happiness, accomplishment, and a blessed old age.

Such "wholesome" honest living created an ethos of responsibility against lying, cheating, stealing, and irresponsibility. It was so ingrained that one would feel ashamed of doing wrong, even if he got away with it. Guilt would punish one more than fines or imprisonment. I still feel terrible if I've made a commitment and for any reason cannot fulfill it. This makes for reliable, dependable relations, if a bit repressed, overly serious, and somewhat boring.

One was to do one's duty according to professional, objective standards, not personal subjective, emotional feelings. It was the unwritten code of "professional" conduct – in business, law, politics, education, and ministry.

I was the youngest child of three, by considerable years. My sister was five years older, and my brother was four years older (this is a long time for children}.   According to the Birth Order Theory of personality, being "the baby" of the family means that I have always seen myself as young. The oldest child is supposedly more adult, as my sister Barbara was, and the middle child is confused (sorry Chuck).

Chuck & Garrett's Airport Outing

Being so much younger, my natural introverted tendencies were magnified by isolation. I always had a few close friends, but

I spent much of my childhood alone, which I liked. Nothing pleased me more than to be curled up with a book, reading. Or watching favorite television shows (*Andy Griffith, Gunsmoke, Bonanza, I Spy,* etc.). I essentially am a loner and enjoy solitary reading, drawing, thinking, walking, and swimming. Team sports never appealed to me – only tennis. And driving alone in my sports car.

The whole secure, stable Midwest social setting was shattered in my 13th year when my family moved to Albuquerque, New Mexico, supposedly for my mother's health (asthma), but was actually my parent's last attempt to salvage their marriage. It didn't work. Within a year they were divorced and soon after that, my mother committed suicide. Her note simply said, "I'm sorry." I felt a strange elation mixed with deep grief at her death.

She was a dear, sweet, innocent Christian lady, brutalized by an unstable bully of a husband. Her trauma, aggravated by alcoholism, addiction to prescription drugs for depression, and misery was finally over and she was in the arms of a loving Savior, Jesus in heaven, where I will meet her, whole, beautiful, and happy.

Some Christians believe that "self-murder" is a mortal sin that leads to hell. The church has traditionally taught that those who kill themselves in madness, insanity, depression, or some other mental affliction (unlike deliberate, premeditated suicide) have not committed a mortal sin and are forgiven, along with every other sin through faith in Christ and His atoning death on the cross.

Before her "illness" (which in reality "took her away" from me by age eight or so) my mother was the sweetest, kindest, smartest, most Christian person I knew. She grew up in the Baptist church and had a simple, loving faith. I remember her tucking me into bed when I was perhaps five years old. She asked me to say my prayers. Like the selfish little body I was, I prayed for more toys for ME; more candy for Me, and for God to side with ME in all my battles. She sweetly said, "That's fine Gary; now let's pray for the poor children who have no toys or candy and for world peace." She was a model of Christian love and charity.

For the next five years in New Mexico (where I found a dry, brown, tacky, busy, ugly Sun Belt city after the green, traditional, calm, and beautiful Wisconsin I'd grown up in). I lived alone with my erratic father as my sister had gone to the University of Michigan and my brother had left home to live with a friend and escape a mean, bullying father. My solitary isolation was especially sweet then.

Because of a couple of inheritances, when I was 19, my brother and I bought a small house and lived contentedly while we both attended the University of New Mexico.

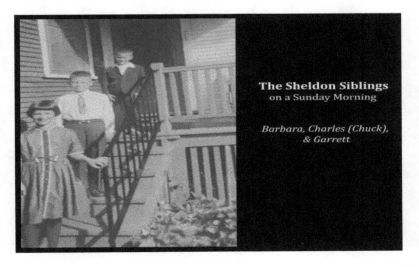

The Sheldon Siblings
on a Sunday Morning

*Barbara, Charles (Chuck),
& Garrett*

EDUCATION

Elementary

As a boy, I walked two miles, through the snow to school. Actually, in Milwaukee, Wisconsin, 1959-1963, it was four one-half mile walks (we walked home for lunch) and during two/third of the school year, there could be snow (sometimes three feet) on the ground (October – March).

My school, Hartford Avenue Elementary, was a small three-story red brick school surrounded by paved playgrounds, built around 1900. It bordered UWM (University of Wisconsin Milwaukee) which at the time was a (primarily) Woman's Teacher's College. My maternal grandmother was Assistant Dean of Women there, so I often walked its hall to visit her. Back then, universities had a "dean of Men" (a man) and a "Dean of Women" (a woman). Not a bad idea, which we might wisely go back to.

On my morning trek to grade school, I usually stopped off at Reigelmann's Drugstore for a candy bar. Usually, I walked alone, but sometimes with friends, including one Jewish boy who veered off at the Synagogue School on the way.

Our last trip home, after the school day, usually involved snowball fights, building snow forts, and sledding. Returning home in the late afternoon our mittens, boots, pants, hat, and coat were soaking wet and freezing. We deposited these clothes on the large cast iron radiator in the entry hall of the house, where they dried for the next day. I was 14 before I learned that numb hands are not normal!

I remember very little in the way of education during kindergarten through 4th grade. I recall kids sitting in a circle on the floor in kindergarten beating on Indian drums. I recall possibly in the first grade, one of many blue-haired matronly teachers reading a story to us. We regularly visited the large school library on the third floor to check out books and gaze out the large, high windows. There, I did my first research paper, when (probably our fourth-grade teacher) put a list of animals on the board and asked us to choose one to write a paper on. I wanted to pick "flying squirrel", but a girl got it before me, so I think I got "gray squirrel". My writing career had begun!

During recess, the boys would form into two large "armies" and conduct "wars" on the playground, stimulating sword fights, etc. Somehow, I was chosen General of one of the armies, which involved running at the front of the boys and leading them into battle. At first, I spent most of the time leading my Force past a cute girl I was trying to impress until one of my Captains said my troops wanted to be led into battle. I always liked the order, decorum, and style of the military (if not the combat) and if I hadn't come of age during the Vietnam War (which was a notorious nightmare) I think I would have happily served in the armed forces.

Middle School

When I was ten, my family, like so many others, moved from the city to the suburbs of Milwaukee, Mequon, which then was mostly rural farms and woods, next to Lake Michigan, about 20 miles north of Milwaukee. I attended Rangeline County School for grades 5-7. Most of the students were farm kids and we now rode a school bus for miles around, through the snow.

Again, I recall little of the education except for my good, funny friends and one teacher, a young, Mr. K. just out of the University of Wisconsin – Madison. He was smart, funny, friendly and kind. The one year I understood math was in his 7th-grade class. He was also a "character", joking with us and coaching the track team (which I ran one year– the 50-yard dash). Once, when he left the room during a test, he looked back through the window in the door, came back into the room, and said, "Why is it that whenever I leave the room, Sheldon, Lawson, and Smith look up?"

This was the age in America with three television channels and every good boy watched the "spy" shows (*Man from Uncle, I Spy*, etc.) and discussed them at school lunch the next day. As boys, we wanted to get out of the school as soon as possible, but as "spies" we would sneak back into the building at recess to see how long we could spy undetected until some teacher would see us and shout, "WHAT are you boys doing HERE?"

Another episode that shows the strict rules of the time was when some friends and I were sitting at the back of the bus making faces at the cars behind us. The next day we were called into a disciplinary hearing of teachers and administrators, questioned, punished, and sent home with notes to our parents. We never made faces out of the school bus window again.

Another boyhood prank was to sit in the back and laugh and talk during class. One particularly tough male teacher in the 5th grade, Mr. G., would throw chalk at us, sometimes hitting us in the head. It was a game to spot the flying chalk before it hit you, raise the school desk lid causing the missile to shatter, sending chalk dust over the room.

Those years (10-13) also began social life with girls: arranged parties and dances under parental supervision: guys' "sleepovers" at each other's houses; and odd flirtations between the boys and girls. But for the most part, boys played with boys and girls with girls.

In 1967, on my 13th birthday, my family moved from Wisconsin to Albuquerque, New Mexico. It was partly for my mother's health (hot, dry Southwestern air was supposed to help her asthma) and my parents' final attempt to salvage their marriage (which didn't work).

The schools in this "Sun Belt" boom town were very different from the close, conservative Midwest culture. The Wisconsin public school teachers were very professional, rigorous, serious, and competent. Albuquerque schools in a booming city with people from all over and a shortage of teachers had a mix of generally good with very bad teachers. One math teacher in high school spent most of the class time in loud hysterics about her personal problems and opinions.

The one outstanding teacher taught senior humanities, looked like a college professor in a tweed jacket and pipe; was highly intellectual and a communist. His passionate, intellectual teaching drew many to his radical view, as others did in my college experience. Revolutionaries can be very captivating.

In New Mexico, I experienced a multicultural society for the first time. In place of the middle-class WASP (White Anglo-Saxon

Protestant) culture of Wisconsin, I meet Hispanic, Native American, American Southern (mostly Texas), and other ethnic groups. The one group that was almost nonexistent was Blacks or African Americans. But I've learned that coming from a "dominant" culture, one (or at least I) didn't really notice or think about the "minority" people.

But they noticed me. My Midwest "accent", style, and manners provoked some responses. Especially the "macho" culture of Hispanic boys seemed offended by my presence. There were very few bullies and fights at Wisconsin schools; there were many in New Mexico. As soon as I arrived in Jr. High School in Albuquerque, I was "picked on" by Hispanic (and sometimes Redneck or Cowboy) youth. Once a group of Mexican boys surrounded me on the playground and one said, "I think you're a Pussy!" This apparently was a challenge to fight, but, not likely to fight, I just replied, "Well, you're entitled to your opinion!"

But, as the bullies' threats became more frequent and ominous I told my father and he enrolled me in karate school, where I studied martial arts for about three years, almost achieving a Green Belt. Just when I felt confident that I could win in any fight, the threats stopped. I think a bully, like a dog, smells fear but also senses confidence and prowess and ceases wanting to fight, knowing they would lose.

I was able to attend karate school because the driving laws were very liberal in New Mexico. At age 14, I believe, you could get a driver's license for a motor scooter with less than 5 hp. I got a Honda 50 and drove myself to school and karate. Then I got a real motorcycle and then a sports car–a *Triumph Spitfire.*

High School

By this time my parents had divorced; my mother was dead; my sister had left for the University of Michigan; and my brother had left home, unable to endure my father's temper. My father was busy with work, his hobbies, and his occasional lady friend, leaving me alone most of the time, to read, think, walk, and draw.

I always was blessed with "guy friends" --buddies who joined me in laughs, pranks, and adventures. Almost no socializing with girls and dating occurred in my public school years, or even in university. I lived in my own world of thoughts, school, some work, and friends.

University

I graduated from Manzano High School in the spring of 1972 and began studying at the University of New Mexico in the summer of 1972 (an Intro-Political Science class). I went as a pre-law student – planning to become a lawyer, as several in my family had. Television law shows like *Perry Mason* and *Judd for the Defense* made it look exciting and rewarding, a combination of detective work and intellectual battles. Also, a prosperous and respected profession. Later when I worked briefly in Real Estate, I saw what most lawyers did: forms and documents – tedious and boring.

But, while I went to UNM as a government major, it was to go to law school. I had always wanted to attend an old Northeastern University for its history, tradition, and prestige; but my father said he would only pay for in-state tuition at a public university, as that's what his father had done.

That University in the 1970s was a charming, exciting place. Built mostly in Indian adobe style, with a large square like an Inca Temple, it had about 20,000 students. Like most major state universities, it had faculty from the best universities like Harvard, Yale, Princeton, and Stanford. So, academically it was as good as an Eastern university.

The warm climate and Spanish-Hispanic culture made it an open, free, casual environment. Every spring they had a "Fiesta": a week-long Mexican-style party all over campus, day and night with music, drinks, food, and dancing. Fun – light and lively!

The large Student Union Building (SUB) had multiple dining halls and cafes where students went between classes to eat, drink, and socialize. My favorite was a second-story outdoor cafe with a grand view of the campus. You would always see some of your classmates, sit and talk. As I told an audience at UNM years later when they presented me with the "Bernard Rodey (Founder of the University) Award for Contributions to Education", I received at least half of my education by drinking tea and socializing at the SUB between classes! We saw old friends and met new ones; talked about our lives, plans, and classes, joked, and laughed.

At one of these conversations, a friend asked if I was in the General Honors Program, as he was. I'd never heard of it. There were departmental honors, if you graduated with a high grade point in your major, but "General" Honors" were not determined by grades but by an Honors Program Board that examined the lengthy written faculty evaluations of your performance in the interdisciplinary seminars. So, although my grades barely justified a *cum laude* (with honors), I graduated *summa cum laude* (with Highest Honors).

The Honors Seminars, like grad classes, met once a week for 2-3 hours, were limited to twelve students, and discussed a book everyone had read that week. I recall a seminar on China: history, culture, literature, food, politics. Fascinating! Once, discussing Chinese Communism, the very old, stodgy professor wore a "Mao cap" during the whole seminar.

The location of the Honors Center was special, being on the ground floor of a large building and containing a large lounge with sunken couches, surrounded by the seminar rooms. We would "hang out" there between classes (when not at the SUB) and talk. It was like a small college of 400 within a large university. I got the best education there (besides meeting my future wife!) and it prepared me for the research seminars and teaching in graduate school. The Honors Director was a physicist from Cambridge University in England and combined British tradition with an almost "hippie-like" radicalism. He called our annual retreats ``advances". He allowed some Honors Seniors to teach a Freshman Honors Seminar! You had to submit a class proposal and it was competitive. Mine was a kind of Western Intellectual History Course (modeled on Jacob Branowski's *Western Intellectual Tradition*) and provided my first teaching experience, which confirmed my calling.

The Honors "College" excellence was later lost in the political correctness that infected all American academia, a new location that looked like a dentist's office, and a mediocre staff. But I was there during "the Golden Age". What a blessing!

I'd come to college with very few political convictions: a vague mix of my family's conservative culture and Republican identities, with some 60-70's Liberalism (Civil Rights, Feminism, Socialism) that emerged in America largely due to protests of the Vietnam War. That war seemed senseless and a frustrating quagmire that played into Marxist/Leninist theories of capitalist imperialism. Also, young people often rebel against whatever their parents stand for, and I embraced the cultural changes of the 1960s – 70's.

However, I was not prepared for the radical "New Left" Communist ideology that swept American higher education. Until I took a Political Theory class taught by a brilliant, passionate, young Marxist professor.

His dynamic personality and charisma for tearing- down the evil, unjust Capitalist system and building a new Socialist utopia of peace, equality, and justice affected me and most of my friends like a strong drug. We became *crusaders* for "The Movement" of impending revolution and Communism. Other young, radical, professors in Philosophy (my minor) and Economics fueled this reforming zeal.

Especially for me, a white-privileged, upper-middle class "bourgeois" male, Marxism could possibly atone for any class sins. My favorite teachers, on whom I later based my own teaching style, were serious, substantive, and organized; but also funny, interesting, and entertaining. I recall my Economic Theory professor, a Communist in the 1930's and now a Liberal Democrat often referring to his (like "my" ancient New England family buried in the town cemetery on a hill above their village, "staring down on us". After handing out the syllabus and introducing the course on the first day, he would announce: "O.K., I'll let you out early, I'm a union man."

Many of my former students, who knew me as a leading Jeffersonian and Burkean Conservative, will be surprised to hear this, but I abandoned my law school plans and prepared for graduate school to get a Ph.D. in Political Theory and become a Marxist professor.

The mistake I made was to get an excellent education. At Rutgers University in New Brunswick, N.J., there were seven

Theorists on the Political Science faculty (where most departments had one or two) representing every period (Ancient Greece and Rome, Middle Ages, Renaissance, Modern, Twentieth Century, Liberalism, Conservatism, Communitarian, Libertarian, etc.).

I soon learned there was a lot more to Political Theory than Marx, Lenin, and Mao. The sublime and brilliant ideas of Plato, Socrates, Aristotle, Cicero, St. Augustine, St. Thomas Aquinas, John Locke, Machiavelli, Hannah Arendt, and Rawls, weaned me away from New Left radicalism. I've been an advocate of comprehensive, balanced, critical debate and academic freedom ever since. And my first textbook, The History of Political Theory: Ancient Greece to Modern American embodies that comprehensive approach (which, sadly, they no longer have) of studying every idea, from every perspective, confident the truth will emerge from a lively free education.

I had applied to six graduate schools, including my "safe" school, the University of Minnesota (because it had just started a Ph.D. program and so needed students!). I was accepted by EVERY school but my "safe school"! My application efforts were greatly helped by the Guide to Graduate Education in Political Science compiled by *The American Political Science Association* which lists every grad program in the U.S. and Canada with department emphasis, faculty degrees and specialties, and admission and Ph.D. requirements. I accepted offers from Rutgers University in New Jersey and the graduate faculty of the New School for Social Research in nearby New York City.

Throughout most of my college years, I shared a house in Albuquerque with my brother Chuck, also a student at UNM. It was a small, lower-middle-class house in a post-WWII sunbelt boom town subdivision called Hoffmantown. He had a bedroom in the front of the house and I in the back which had a small addition for my "study" – making it like rooms at an Oxford College staircase.

When I graduated, we sold the house, the proceeds from which financed my first year of graduate school. He went on to a graduate degree in anthropology and a career in the military. Our college years together made a lasting bond between my brother and me.

Graduate School

In the summer of 1977, I graduated from the University of New Mexico (without attending commencement graduation ceremonies – which were not "cool", especially for a radical student). My brother and I had sold our little house to an aged brother and sister who recently retired from Loyola University, Chicago.

With the proceeds, and "all my worldly goods" (dozens of books and a little furniture) I loaded up a U-Haul trailer and pulled it behind my 1967 Volvo 122S (a medium-sized sedan that resembled a 1930's American car). I went to Whitefish Bay, Wisconsin, and visited my beloved NaNa.; unloaded my belongings in her garage; and drove to our family cottage in Michigan. Then I went back to Wisconsin; reloaded my possessions; and proceeded to New England: Warwick, Rhode Island, and my sister and brother-in-law's house. They had a small Cape Cod house near the ocean with a perfect guest room, with a bath and a nearby kitchen.

That was my "base of operations" that summer, from which I made 200-mile excursions to New Jersey and New York to set up my digs for impending grad school. The people of New Jersey I found them as blunt and rude (obviously not polite Midwesterners) and the rents are exorbitant. Getting off the New Jersey Turnpike, I asked the toll booth attendance which way to turn to get to Rutgers. He yelled: "Do I look like a f____ tour guide! "

But, by the grace of God, I found an ad in the local newspaper for a loft/attic apartment above a small house in Edison, N.J., about four miles north of Rutgers. This one-room apartment was owned by an elderly Jewish couple, Germans who had escaped Nazi Germany in the 1940's. They were courteous and finally, almost like family: step-grandparents. What a blessing to have privacy for $150 a month within walking distance of the university. I think back then I lived on about $400 a month!

Still, it was scary to be embarking, alone, on a new "career" in a strange place. When I left Barbara and Bill's house in late summer, he said, "You're welcome here anytime for any length of time." That family love and hospitality meant everything to me! It provided security as I entered an uncertain world that gave me the confidence to take risks, including getting a Ph.D. in a very uncertain job market.

At Rutgers, an old 1766 Eastern "Ivy League" Colonial College – now state university, in New Brunswick, New Jersey. The new political science graduate students had the orientation session at Eagleton Institute, an old antebellum mansion on the Douglas College Campus, headquarters to the program that trained M.P.A. students for government service. The director opened the proceedings by saying, "Here at Rutgers, we have two Political Science graduate programs: one that leads to the Ph.D. and one that leads to employment."

I was informed that I must choose a "major" field out of the five or six in the Pol-Sci and two "minor" fields. My major was Political Theory and my minors were American Politics and Constitutional Law. Five years later, I would have a five-hour written Comprehensive Exam in each of my minors and a two-hour "Oral" Exam in my major (with five faculty members asking me questions). It was a brutal experience!

Most of us took 2-4 graduate seminars a semester that were extremely rigorous and demanding: Reading (1-3 books a week; in-class presentations/discussions, and 30-50 page research papers.) It was much more intense than undergraduate school. Some students quickly cracked under the strain and left.

Ironically, one thing that kept me going (and sane) was more reading – but light fiction, usually before bed, to relax. I preferred 19th-century English and American authors, good writers and humorous writers like Mark Twain, Nathaniel Hawthorne, Anthony Trollop, and late Edwardians like P.G. Wodehouse and John Mortimer.

A small circle of student-friends kept us going with encouragement, camaraderie, shared suffering, and fun. About ten of us met weekly at one of our apartments supposedly to discuss a reading, but really to drink Molson's Ale, joke, and laugh, relieving the stress of graduate school. At one point, we decided our group should have a name. "Political Theory Study Group" seemed too pompous. Then one evening at a department banquet for a visiting dignitary, our graduate chairman, a prominent scholar of American Political Parties and Elections, was boasting to our guest of the world-famous faculty at Rutgers. Even though most of our graduate students are pretty "Schlocky"' (a Yiddish term that is not very complimentary). So, we instantly became "The Schlocks". Those Schlocks went on to many academic positions, honors, and scholarships, and still met at conferences for a "Schlock Dinner".

The graduate Political Science faculty at Rutgers was indeed one of the best in the country, with world-renowned scholars in American Politics, Comparative and International Politics, and Constitutional Law, and from universities like Harvard, Yale, Princeton, Columbia, and Berkeley. At that time, Rutgers, like Oxford, was made up of several small colleges: Rutgers College (the original men's college for Dutch Reformed clergy) Douglass College, the Women's College; Livingston College, a modern 1950s "progressive" college north of New Brunswick; Cook College, the Agricultural School; and Busch Campus (medical). These were all "united" in the early 1980's to imitate the large state universities like Wisconsin so the distinctive faculties of the separate small colleges were brought together in one location (my department in a modern high-rise office building near the Douglass campus).

But that was one reason we had so many Political Theorists —each College had one or two, so combined, we had seven representing any period and field (Ancient, Medieval, Liberalism, Renaissance, Marxism, Communitarian, Conservation, etc.). I learned every period and ideology from all perspectives, leading to my appreciation of Academic Freedom, debate, discussion of all views, learning, and my first book: *The History of Political Theory: Ancient Greece to Modern America.*

It was a challenging, intense, difficult, exciting, and exhausting time. As I recently told someone, it was so rich, that my six years at Rutgers provided me with twenty years of ideas to work out in my teaching and scholarship. The professors were all distinctive personalities. Benjamin B., a prominent Communitarian Theory scholar was long-haired, flamboyant, and artsy (living near the Theatre District in New York City and writing plays): Gordon S., a Cambridge-educated British Liberalism scholar who routinely showed up an hour late but "made it us to us" by keeping us two hours over. A wealthy and elegant Renaissance scholar; an angry German Critical Theory scholar; and one I still keep in touch with, Professor Myron Aronoff who taught Political Culture, especially of Israel. And my favorite, as a mentor, Cary McWilliams, about whom I'll say much more later.

The New School for Social Research

During my first year at Rutgers, I also took classes at The Graduate Faculty of the New School for Social Research, in a small office building in Manhattan, right in Greenwich Village, New York City. This had been established in the 1930s as the University in Exile for Jewish intellectuals fleeing Nazi persecution. It still had a very European flavor. I recall a philosophy course taught by a German professor – very strict and brilliant. At the end of the term, preparing to write research papers, a student asked, "Professor, do you think a study could be made of Marx and Weber?" After squinting his eyes and thinking, he replied, "*Yes...I zink zo.*" The student said, "How would one go about doing that?" The haughty professor replied, "READ THEM! SIT IN A CHAIR!!!"

After a year it was clear I could not do both schools and discontinued the New School, transferring my credits to Rutgers. But the year I rode the train or bus into NYC from New Brunswick was precious. "The City '' then was the most exciting place in the world. Millions of people from all over the world; giant skyscrapers, and every kind of shop, restaurant, museum, school, or church. At Christmas, the top of the Empire State Building was lit in red and green. I ate at "Famous Ray's Pizza" – standing in a line that wrapped around the block, for a delicious slice of pizza the size of half a pizza for about $2.00. I saw people and things I'd never imagined in Wisconsin!

Constant beggars, yelling cab drivers, rich and poor, every ethnic group from around the world rushing about the crowded sidewalks. No place is more thrilling for a boy in his mid-20s. At times frightening. Crime was high in the 1970's especially in the subway. My constant "weapon", rain or shine, was a large umbrella. My father's advice in dangerous situations *"Never show fear"* came in handy.

One summer night I missed the subway stop at Columbia University, where I was a graduate intern in the scholarly journal *Political Theory,* and popped up in the middle of a very crowded, hot, and hostile-looking Harlem. Threatening stares went unobserved as I "calmly" walked back into the subway station...I will always cherish that year in New York. Now, I would not go there for a million dollars!

But Rutgers had plenty to keep me occupied. After my first year, I received a Teaching Assistantship which paid my tuition and gave me about $3000 income a year. We would attend assigned undergraduate classes, do grading, and lead 'Recitations'-- seminars on Fridays after the Professor did Monday and Wednesday. My final year was blessed with a Fellowship of $5000 a year and NO teaching duties. This was perfect because that year I was taking my Ph.D. Comprehensive Exams and writing my doctoral dissertation. I married Elaine in 1980 and we lived in married student housing at Princeton Theological Seminary where she attended.

Those 2 ½ years in Princeton are a blur, as I did nothing but study and write. Occasionally, I would go into town and shop, eat at the Princeton dining hall, or browse at the university bookstore where I had more preppy clothes than books. In a nearby small town of Cranberry was an old bookstore – *The Cranberry Bookworm* occupying a big old colonial house and having hundreds of old books bought from estate sales in the area. I joined Nassau Presbyterian Church.

It was a joke that to prepare for these "Comps" students would do some "strange things" to force the at-home exile to study 10-14 hours a day. One friend shaved half his head to be too embarrassed to go out. Another hid all his clothes.

Those exams were grueling, but I passed all the first time, by the grace of God. I told everyone my written essays with an italic-tip fountain pen were illegible but looked too good to flunk. The two-hour "Oral Comprehensive" with five Political Theory scholars asking ME questions was also a blur, but I passed. One friend of mine froze in fear and flunked. He passed the second time. Then the 300-page doctoral dissertation of original scholarship. I did mine on "Classical and Modern Influences in Political Theory of Thomas Jefferson", showing the Ancient Greek and British liberal strains in that Founder. In a very tight job market, the joke at Rutger was, "What is Sheldon going to do with a dissertation on Jefferson? Go to Virginia"? This is exactly what I did, fulfilling a dream to (a) live in a rural area, (b) live in Virginia (c) be associated with "Mr. Jefferson's University "(UVA), and (d) teach at a small liberal arts college.

I got it all!

Those years in graduate school at Rutgers in the late 1970s/early 1980s were Golden: demanding, hard, frustrating, scary, fun, exciting, and exhilarating. As I wrote upon retiring *"What Made America Academia Great and How It Was Destroyed"* (*American Greatness,* June 2019), later published as "The Decline and Fall of the University", that was a by-gone era of academic freedom, debate, and argument. Learning to THINK, ANALYZE, CREATE that twenty years later was sacrificed on the altar of Political correctness, censorship, speech codes, Title IX, Inclusion, Diversity, Equity identity politics, and mediocrity.

The academy of that era had a professionalism, a code of intellectual quality, and honesty that we have lost in American higher education. And that has hurt progress in economics, technology, politics, and morality.

And it wasn't that the professors or departments were perfect. They were arrogant, vain, proud, pompous, petty, and at times, foolish. But they adhered to a standard of research, debate, intellectual honesty, and integrity that has been largely corrupted by politics, interest groups, and P.R. marketing.

I recall being called back into the conference room after "defending" my dissertation (the last act before getting the Ph.D.) and the senior faculty member greeting me, shaking my hand, and saying "Congratulations, DR. Sheldon". It was a Rite of Passage signifying joining the ranks of the academician. You were now expected to be like them: hard-working, reputable, serious about your subject, collegial, and CONTRIBUTING to the world of scholarship as they had. When I was opening my defense with an outline of my dissertation on the chalkboard, so they "could follow my argument" my advisor said, "We don't 'follow', your arguments, Sheldon, we 'experience' them." I drove home in a daze to Princeton where my wife had a banner and display of CONGRATULATIONS for me.

It all reflected the spirit of community both academic and social that ruled the university in those days and I hope that we regain some day. Brilliant, eccentric professors, funny, weird students; a complex and almost incomprehensible system. But the *social life* made it special and relationships cut through the bureaucracy. Not only fellow students, but also faculty, staff, and students socialized together, partied together, and drank at pubs together. It was personal and fun. But now, with the fear of "harassment", or "offending someone", and political correctness, almost all of that, along with the humor is gone.

It was a blessing to be a part of it, for which I will always be grateful.

While studying, writing, teaching, and trying to remain sane, the last couple of years of graduate school were also spent applying for jobs. The academic market in higher education in the 1980s was tight, but nothing like today, where there are thousands of applicants for every position, amid declining enrollments and budgets, hiring freezes, online universities, and general disregard for compromised universities.

I was fairly typical in having three interviews: with a private elite college in New England, a public university in the South, and a small liberal arts college, a branch of the University of Virginia, in the rural Appalachian mountains called Clinch Valley College. The latter had an ad for an Assistant Professor of Political Science in The Chronicle of Higher Education that I saw while sitting in the Department Chair's reception area waiting to see him. I jotted down the address, typed a cover letter, and sent off my resume' (vitae). I got a call from the Dean almost immediately, inviting me for an interview in November 1982. I was to defend my dissertation the following month. I got the job and started in Wise, Virginia in January of 1983.

Living in Princeton, I flew out of the airport in Philadelphia to Charlotte, North Carolina, and then up to the small regional Tri-Cities Tennessee airport.

There was a low cloud covering and our small plane flew under the clouds. I had a window seat and marveled at the view of gorgeous, rugged, tree-covered mountains, some with deep blue lakes in them. I'd never witnessed such natural beauty before. I fell in love with the region before we landed.

At the airport, I was greeted by the College Dean and Department Chair (unheard of today when an applicant would be told to rent a car and drive up). That was the informal, friendly atmosphere of the day. I was asked if I could teach four courses a semester, covering American Politics, State and Local Politics, Public Administration, Constitutional Law, and Political Theory. I assented, though I hadn't actually studied a couple of those subjects!

It reminded me of when C.S. Lewis interviewed at Magdalen College, Oxford, and he was asked if he could teach Philosophy and Political Theory as well as Literature he said in his *Memoir* he would have said he could teach Zoology if they'd asked him, just to get the job.

I stayed at the old Inn at Wise and had breakfast in the old dining room watching "local old boys" talking and laughing over their coffee, looking like Mayberry. I met many staff and faculty at CVC during my interview. All were friendly and welcoming. After a literally COLD interview in New England, this was a nice change. I don't remember what my "Guest Lecture" was about, but the students were happy and lively, laughing at all my jokes. One or two people I met were bores, but most including the Dean's elegant secretary (with a charming voice and Southern accent) were very nice and attractive. I fell in love with the area and the people. I felt at home. It was not the most prestigious place I'd interviewed, but I felt drawn there and never regretted it.

TEACHING

Describing an almost 40-year career at an institution from which I retired just a year ago is not easy. But I felt drawn to this small college in the remote mountains of Southwest Virginia; had a fascinating and blessed life there; and will try to hit some of the "highlights" to illustrate what a special place it was. Especially since it has been altered tremendously during the past few years and soon may no longer exist.

"Clinch Valley College " (of the University of Virginia), later "The University of Virginia's College at Wise" was begun in 1954 (the same year I began). It is situated in the rugged and beautiful mountains of the Appalachian Range in Virginia, near Kentucky and Tennessee.

It was a very isolated region when first settled in the late 1700s, almost inaccessible; and still is a very remote, out-of-the-way place. Someone once told me the earliest settlers were indentured servants (probably "Scots-Irish") who stepped off their English ships and "hit the ground running", not stopping until they reached a rugged, wild area hidden from the rest of the world. They were subsistence farmers, "hillbillies", who survived with corn, hunting, fishing, and "moonshine" liquor (animated by "old-time, bluegrass music" on fiddles, mandolins, and jugs. } One thinks of "*The Darling Family*" on the *Andy Griffith Show.*

The discovery of coal in the late 1800s led to the railroad entering and local men becoming miners. The Appalachian culture reminded one of that in Ireland: close families, community, strong religious faith, humorous storytelling, friendliness, and fierce independence. I felt immediately at home here–with the scenery of deep green wooded mountains, broad green valleys, deep blue sky, and bright white clouds. Intoxicatingly beautiful. Years later, when I visited my family homeland in England, the Northern Midlands looked much like my new home.

I was introduced to mountain culture shortly after arriving in Wise County when my old Jaguar car, with a broken fuel gauge, ran out of gas on a hot summer day on my way to the College. Standing by the stranded car, I soon saw a car pull over in front of mine. A middle-aged woman got out and asked what was wrong. I explained I had run out of gas. She offered to get me some. When she returned, she handed me the gas can and a cold drink because "I looked hot and thirsty". It thought I'd died and gone to heaven. The Good Samaritan – that Christian spirit of helping anyone in need (or correcting anyone in error). I have seen this many times since.

Clinch Valley College came out of that local spirit. In the early 1950s most local kids could never attend college, even at "nearby" Radford College or Virginia Tech (160 miles away) for the expense and travel involved. One wintry evening, at the old Inn at Wise, an extension agent for the University of Virginia met a few prominent citizens to offer courses in the area. The locals, later known as *"The Three Wise Men"* asked for a local college instead, and traveled to Charlottesville and Richmond to get approval, and $5000, for the first two years of operation.

They acquired the old county *Poor Farm:* a big stone building on about 200 acres outside the town of Wise. Another stone building nearby that had been a *Baptist Home for Wayward Girls* was turned into a women's dormitory.

The surrounding community supported the 2-year junior college (feeder for UVA) with gifts, money, volunteer work, and enthusiasm. I remember my office had beautiful light oak bookcases and a wooden file cabinet donated by local furniture stores.

In the mid-1970s "CVC" became a four-year liberal arts college branch of the University of Virginia. It was so small it was more like a "twig" than a branch. But for most of the next 40 years, it had about 2000 students and built new classrooms and office buildings, a library, dorms, and a science complex. A row of small houses formed *"Faculty Row"* for new teachers, as housing was still scarce in the area. A modest but enthusiastic beginning.

By the time I came to the college in the mid-1980s, it had about 100 faculty, mostly from regional universities from Kentucky, Tennessee, North Carolina, and Georgia. The best had Ph.D.s from our *sister* institution, the University of Virginia in Charlottesville. Most of the students were still from the surrounding area, but as the coal industry and local population declined, more students were drawn from all over Virginia and over America and the world.

Most of the college staff were from the surrounding counties of Wise, Lee, Scott, and Dickenson and attended the college. This confirmed the informal "family" feeling of the place.

In the year 2000, the most momentous event happened since its founding in 1954. The Commonwealth of Virginia changed the college's name from Clinch Valley College of the University of Virginia to "The University of Virginia's College at Wise". This was the academic equivalent of winning the billion-dollar lottery!

At that time "UVA" was the top "Public Ivy" in the country: a publicly supported but "Ivy League" quality institution like Harvard, Yale, and Princeton. The University of Virginia's founding by American Founder Thomas Jefferson, its classical architecture and lawn, and world-class faculty and programs, meant that to share its name was a jackpot.

The understanding was that the college deliberately raised standards and quality: in Admissions, Faculty, Research, Facilities, and reputation. And we did so, and the college flourished in enrollment, programs, faculty publication, rankings, and benefactors. Financial giving and endowments grew rapidly. New dorms, labs, programs, lectureships, professorships, and sports programs boomed. It was the *Golden Age* for about 10 years.

An excitement and dynamism grew under the leadership of UVA President, John T. Casteen III, and his colleague, Chancellor Jay Lemons.

Clubs and societies flourished. A positive, exciting academic and social environment prevailed. It was like being in the early years of Harvard College: intellectual excellence with a lively, fun community.

Several autumns in that Golden Age of 2000-2010 the entering class was so large (even with heightened admissions requirements) that the college had to buy apartment buildings in town to house them. There was a shortage of classroom space for all the new courses during the "prime times" of mid-morning to mid-afternoon and faculty were forced to schedule early morning and evening classes.

This wonderful time in the history of the college began to decline around 2011 and fell into deep decline after 2014. The University in Charlottesville also began to slip in quality due to political correctness, and Title IX violations of academic freedom. General mismanagement and incompetence spread throughout the Administration. The UVA-Wise enrollment, along with quality began to decline, sometimes by 100-200 students a year, so that now it is 50% below the standard 2000 students it had always had. Financial decline followed. Cuts in staff and programs. Worse, a decline in morale and that positive, happy spirit that had prevailed since the college's founding.

The reasons for this sad decline are obviously complex. Nationally, university enrollment is down. Regional schools competed for students; social demographics, and even the COVID-19 virus all contributed to the loss of a fine institution.

But failed leadership, mismanagement, and incompetence cannot be ruled out of the equation. As I wrote in my academic "Swan Song" upon retiring, *What Made American Academia Great and How It Was Destroyed*; republished as "The Decline and Fall of the University", when an emphasis on academics, freedom of speech, debate, and social interaction is replaced with political agendas of liberal political correctness, Title IX, Inclusion, Diversity, and Identity Politics (and then remedied with Public Relations and Marketing slogans and gimmicks), an institution of higher education is going to suffer.

This affected the college in the summer of 2014 when the Obama Department of Education expanded the Title IX law on discrimination to include every aspect of academic and social life. Professor Laura Kipnis's book "Unwanted Advances" is the best summary of the efforts of these regulations (that were overturned in 2020) turning open, free, lively, and pleasant universities into police states, and the horrors of surveillance, interrogation, and arbitrary judgments and punishments.

An atmosphere of fear and persecution prevailed. By 2016 this had even affected UVA-Wise, where students and faculty were afraid to speak, act, or laugh for fear of being accused of offending someone and investigated, adjudicated, and expelled or dismissed by the Office of Conduct and Compliance. I composed a Resolution on Academic Freedom for the Faculty Senate (see "Virginia Professors Champion Freedom of Speech" THE COLLEGE FIX) which passed unanimously to little effect.

I was never personally charged or investigated, as far as I know, but I knew faculty and students who were. It poisoned the whole atmosphere. By 2016 three years before I formally retired: I had in effect "retired" — only giving lectures, and perfunctory office hours and then going home. The academic and social life of the College was dead.

However, before these last years, the College and I enjoyed an exciting, fulfilling, and prosperous time.

Like most new teachers, I spent most of my time outside of class preparing for the next class! We usually were one chapter ahead of the students. Teaching four courses a semester (two of which I'd never studied: Public Administration and State and Local Politics) with office hours, committees, and department meetings, every spare moment was spent in class preparation. For my first two years, it was constant. Gradually, as the course lectures were formed, I could take some time off from school -work: first Sundays, then a few evenings a week, then Saturdays.

Once your class lectures were "set" you could focus more on research, writing, and publishing. The old adage of the university professor, *"publish or perish"*, not get tenure, applied even at CVC. So, my third or fourth summer, a Summer Research Grant freed me from teaching summer school, and I wrote my first book: *The History of Political Theory: Ancient Greece to Modern America.*

This was a textbook that came out of my Rutgers and CVC survey call on Classics of Political Thought (Plato, Aristotle, Cicero, St. Augustine, Aquinas, Machiavelli, Locke, Marx, etc.) I had outlined the book whilst teaching the course, so putting it together was fairly quick work. I'd take my morning tea, writing pad, and notes out to a chaise in the backyard and write for 4-5 horses straight. I don't have that stamina now when I'm good for about an hour and a half.

The book had two distinctive features: it examined each thinker's view of (1.) Human Nature (2.) Political Society, and (3.) Social Ethics; and it quoted heavily from the original writings. This made it easier to COMPARE the great thinkers. I'd gotten the idea for this approach while in grad school at Rutgers and floated it by a prominent professor who said it could not be done. It's been in print for 33 years.

A small European scholarly press based in Berne, Switzerland, Peter Lang Publishers, printed it from the original typescript in 1988. Lang was known for small printings of obscure scholarly works (often doctoral dissertations) mostly for university libraries. Mine has been in print for 33 years and used in my *History of Political Theory* course. One of the most gratifying aspects has been students in other fields of Science, Business, English, etc.; said it made the subject interesting to them. Also, the occasional email from a student in another country who ran across it in their university library, and helped in a term paper on Locke or Marx or Freud. An entire new edition of this classic is being published next year: THE NEW HISTORY OF POLITICAL THEORY: Ancient Greece to the Modern World.

My next book, The Political Philosophy of Thomas Jefferson (John Hopkins University Press) was a revision of my Rutgers doctoral dissertation, a professional expectation. It took eight years to get published and rejected by at least 70 universities and academic presses before being accepted by John Hopkins. The review process for scholarly books is a brutal process with editors, readers, revisions, and rejections. Much of the process is unfair and you develop a very thick skin. Perseverance is necessary. That book was followed by the *Political Philosophy of James Madison; Religion and Politics: Major Thinkers on Church and State; An Encyclopedia of Political Thought*; and numerous book chapters, conference papers, journal articles, and book reviews.

This scholarship and good teaching evaluations led to the college nominating me for "The Outstanding Faculty in Virginia Award:" the highest honor given to an academic by the Commonwealth of Virginia. Most awards in this world are political and biased. This was a "real" award: 100 nominees for all Virginia colleges and universities out of about 14,000 faculty and given to ten. I was the first professor at CVC to receive it. That contributed to my getting early tenure and then an endowed professorship. Tenure is a system for teachers, like Federal Judges, to have permanent employment to protect academic freedom (teaching controversial subjects) as judicial independence is for judges. It provided job security for life, barring professional misconduct, criminal convictions, or "moral turpitude". It freed you to work without worry of being fired for personal or political reasons.

The Endowed Chair is a private- fund donated to supplement your public position and salary as a reward for past scholarly performance and an incentive for future performance. My *John Morton Beaty Professorship* was named for a prominent businessman and State Senator by his three elderly daughters with about a million dollars. This freed me to teach strictly within my field and two courses a term instead of four, to have a summer stipend to free me from teaching summer school (to do more writing) and a semester sabbatical leave every five years, to be a visiting scholar at Oxford University, the University of Vienna, Austria, and Trinity College, Dublin Ireland. The travel budget allowed one to study and speak in Moscow, Istanbul, Australia, and Israel. All of this led to more scholarship and prestige for the college.

Most endowed professorships are given by universities to up-and-coming faculty who are getting noticed and job offers from other institutions. It is a way to attract and retain high-quality faculty. With the rise of online education, adjunct (part-time) teachers, and higher education cutbacks, both tenured and endowed chairs are going by the wayside to the disadvantage of education.

Mine was the first endowed chair at the college. A friend said, "Congratulations, next time it might be a couch!"

Until recently, there were a large number of social organizations at UVA-Wise clubs, societies, fraternities, sororities, intra-collegiate sports, and professional associations. These have declined with enrollment, disappeared, or been absorbed by the college under the control of central administration. In a totalitarian society, they don't encourage private groups but put everything under state control. The Boy Scouts became *The Hitler Youth* in Nazi, Germany and *The Communist Youth League* in the Soviet Union.

During most of my career at the college there was a lively variety of student clubs chartered by the institution, enjoying much independence and freedom. In *political theory,* this is called *Civil Society.* It makes for a fun and interesting community. I recall the BSU (Baptist Student Union} under the wonderful campus minister Jim Collie. In a building adjoining the campus the *Center of Christ Life* thrived there for over 30 years. Students of all denominations (AND non-Christians) met, studied, socialized, prayed, sang, and enjoyed wonderful fellowship.

The "main event" was the Wednesday evening (5 p.m.) dinner and program. The hall was packed with 60-70 students – eating, laughing, praying and singing. Usually, a musical program or speaker followed the meal and then most would stay around for two to three more hours just socializing.

A lot of ministry took place during the BSU (later BCM – Baptist Collegiate Ministry) and lifelong friendships were made. I served as a Faculty Advisor for over 20 years and planned my whole schedule around its activities!

When Jim (the most gifted, loving, wise, and accessible campus minister I've ever known) retired, an era ended. A very gifted interim campus minister, a singer, and a teacher from my own church continued the fine tradition of the BSU. But she didn't have a seminary degree and the Virginia Baptist Association in Richmond, which funded the ministry, wanted such.

A very promising-looking young couple was hired. The man immediately began making drastic changes, because he was "in charge", including canceling the Wednesday night dinners. I pleaded with him to give it a chance, for one semester, and see how wonderful it was. I had BSU students in my office crying about the changes and destruction of this beloved institution. But within a couple of years, it was finished, destroyed by poor leadership, and never recovered. Heartbreaking!

But I've seen other organizations (civic, religious, academic) similarly decline from greatness to obscurity in a very short time due to inept leadership. It can take 30 years to build up an institution and one year to destroy it. "Rome wasn't built in a day; but it fell in one hour.", as the saying goes.

Other less stupendous organizations have come and gone. A small group of us young professors formed "The Junior Faculty Caucus" that met on weekends to talk, laugh, and drink beer. When I was promoted and tenured, a Chancellor asked how I could still be involved in the J.F.C. since I was not a senior faculty member. I said, "I was a founder, so now I'm an honorary member". That only lasted about six or seven years.

I formed the Faculty Colloquium, modeled on our Departmental Colloquium at Rutgers where a professor would give a talk on his or her research to faculty colleagues, followed by questions and discussion. It was an informal, fun but very academic activity. At one presentation by a science professor on his research on beavers in Northern Michigan an old history professor asked, "Would you describe them as busy?"

That lasted about ten years before a new administration first removed me as head and then abolished it.
Other clubs that I advised were the Pre-Law Society (or Juris Society) for students planning to go to Law School; a debate club called The Socratic Society; and various political and philosophical clubs. Many of them sponsored important public debates, led by prominent people and attended by large audiences.

When we left "Faculty Row' my wife, Elaine, and I became "Dorm Parents" of a new apartment complex dubbed "The Honors House". This was a dorm of about 60 students, serious and orderly. Most were on the Honor Roll Dean's List. It was self-selecting and self-governing by an Honor House Council and for three years it was a clean, quiet, orderly, studious, and fun residential community. No drugs, loud music, or wild behaviors. I recall returning to our apartment at 11 pm one night to see all the lights on and so quiet you could hear a pin drop. We had socials, croquet-on-the-lawn, parties, but all were very mature and civilized. The presence of a faculty couple IN the dorm set a tone of adulthood and academics.

It was widely criticized for being "elitist". When we moved out Elaine was expecting our first child, it was quickly abandoned by the College Administration and absorbed into standard student housing.

But the H.H. was an experiment in a self-governing, academic dorm with resident faculty that worked.

Other interesting College activities included a TV show on the College television station called *Thoughts and Talk* modeled on William F. Buckley's *Firing Line* and a C-Span taping of one of my political theory lectures. The College Communications Department had a television station on the local cable network but rarely broadcast anything except the occasional sports event or official speech. I suggested a College TV station might have academic programming. This was met with some suspicion and even hostility, but eventually, I tried *UVA-Wise Thoughts and Talk* on YouTube involving my interviewing a faculty member on his/her research. It employed like Buckley's *Firing Line*, a casual, Socratic questioning and discussion.

I recall a good one in 2012 with Economics Professor David Kendall discussing his new book on *Capitalism and Morality*. Also, Dr. Wendy Welch and her book about *The Little Bookstore of Big Stone Gap*. All were fun and informative and widely viewed in the area. I even had a theme at the program's beginning and end: a movement of Haydn's *"Farewell" Symphony* (as Buckley had a Bach piece).

But the technical support (scheduling, editing, taping, broadcasting) was so unreliable that I finally just gave it up.

A few years later, C-Span taped one of my History of Political Theory lectures ("John Rawls and American Liberalism") which was widely broadcast in 2018, and received a lot of attention.

My favorite part of the 2-camera approach: one on me lecturing and one on the students in the class. This was back when a professor could be serious but still, kid around, make jokes, etc. The student's facial expressions and questions capture the best of college teaching at a liberal arts institution: fun, small, personal, and familiar.

That close, warm atmosphere was largely destroyed by the expansion of the Title IX Law in 2014. Supposed to destroy sexual harassment and assault, it destroyed Freedom of Speech and therefore, education. The key was "verbal harassment" which is defined as any talk, expression, laugh, or action that was unwelcomed, unwanted, disliked, or offended someone.

Everyone, especially women, gays, and minorities could report any remark, attitude, conduct, appearance, behavior, or person that they found objectionable and that would trigger an investigation, interrogation, adjudication, (without Due Process of Law: rights of evidence, witnesses, a notice of charges, cross-examination} but judgment, punishment, expulsion, termination, warning, and re-education, etc.

The effect of this subjective and arbitrary was a "chilling effect" on all communication for fear of being charged under Title IX to the Office of Conduct, Compliance, Diversity, and Inclusion. I never was a victim of these draconian tactics, but I know faculty and students who were and it was horrifying.

This was often referred to as the "weaponizing" or "politicizing" of a law against discrimination. Hundreds of court cases overturned these violations of academic freedom and legal procedure, and the U.S. Department of Education corrected most of the abuses in the new Title IX Guidelines in 2020.

But the damage has been done. Educational and social life had been ruined. Everyone (especially old, white males) was afraid to speak for fear of "offending" someone and being hauled before a KGB-style inquisition. I later realized that this, in effect, gave every individual a "veto" over what every other person said: universal censorship.

Where students and faculty used to talk and joke casually, the offices and college campus became a ghost town, a graveyard of fear and silence. Tragically, the real victims of this policy were minorities and women whom for years I had mentored with academic and professional information and advice. My (and other) offices were always full of students, chatting, joking, and being friends as well as colleagues. Amid personal stories and laughter, a lot of politics, history, philosophy, and theology were discussed.

Consequently, I could almost always get my students into the best graduate schools, law schools, and jobs, because I could write a personal recommendation, highlighting some challenges overcome in their lives, or accomplishments, learned from these conversations.

A few students, mostly bright, confident young men still valued open, free discussion, and I was able to mentor them, leading to a highlight of my career: A Retirement Roast!

A particularly bright senior, Eric Daoust, got together about twelve of my favorite students, past and present, to "Roast" me in the Gray Room at the Inn at Wise, the last month of my career.

If you ever saw a Dean Martin Roast on TV, it involves a person being insulted, and teased, but appreciated and honored by friends and colleagues. Then the" Roasted" gets to "Roast" his "Roasters". What fun and dream of every teacher to be honored by one's favorite students: the greatest reward you can get.

I recall Eric Daoust (the Roastmeister) opening the two-hour session by saying, "Professor Sheldon is known as a Burkean Conservative but that's only because he hasn't updated his lecture notes in 30 years!" It went downhill from there. But intermingled with good-natured teasing and witty insults was a love, respect, and adoration that touched the heart. Again, every academic's dream is to be honored by one's students. It was also special that my son and a dear friend, Phil Henry were there.

Afterwards, we took pictures and celebrated. I will never forget it and am deeply grateful for the memory.

That Retirement Roast and the Students Awards a week later were a fitting conclusion to my teaching career. At the Awards celebration (mercifully small and brief) many of the students I'd nominated received "Best Government Major" or "Best Pre-Law Student Awards. Afterward, we gathered for group pictures.

I'd give each of my majors a book reflecting their interests from my library: Conservatism, Communism, Libertarianism, Christianity.

The was the best of small college life: serious but fun, friendly, community. Hopefully, higher education will return someday to the exciting, free, open learning environment I knew and loved, which led to progress in economics, technology, politics, and society. The purpose and result of such a rigorous but open-free atmosphere of learning, debate, discussion, investigation, and community was to teach one to think, reason, and understand. That's what "higher" education in the liberal arts tradition going back to ancient Athens meant.

Once people learned to reason, they could solve new problems, create new solutions, and innovate. So, the quality of education in a country affects the quality of many other institutions and practices in that country, the happiness of the citizens, and the quality of democracy.

I feel blessed that I had an academic career when the university was lively, challenging, and fun!

RESEARCH AND PUBLICATIONS

The old academic adage "Publish or Perish" refers to the fact that to get tenure and keep one's job in a college or university, a professor had to do scholarly publishing (in a book by an academic or university press or professional "refereed" journal articles). This created much stress for the young academics as such publishing had to occur in the first six years (before tenure evaluation) when one was also busy preparing class lectures, serving on committees, attending conferences, trying to live, etc.

My College had minor requirements for scholarly publication (a Letter to the Editor of the local newspaper *The Coalfield Progress* would probably do) but most universities required a book with a prominent University Press that is well-reviewed in professional journals or three articles/book chapters in scholarly journals or books.

At the time it affected me, a great debate was going on about "Teaching" versus "Research." The idea was that we (CVC) were a teaching institution focusing on instruction, advising, and serving students . . . Major research universities emphasized research, discovery, and major contributions to one's field. I always thought that this was at best a false dichotomy and, at worst, an excuse not to read a book. Without ongoing study and research, one's teaching grew stale and uninspiring. It was easy, after gaining tenure, to kick back, give one's old lectures, and relax. Manuscript reviews and conference presentations are hard and challenging (sometimes humiliating). But you have to keep up your scholarship to be a good teacher and do close teaching to inspire good research.

This all changed when Political Correctness and Indoctrination overtook Academic Freedom and Standards. Now you just need to have the right attitude and identity.

My first scholarly publication was a textbook: *The History of Political Theory: Ancient Greece to Modern America*, published by a small European (Swiss) Academic Press, Peter Lang Publishers. By traditional standards, a text was not a scholarly publication. But it came out of my ten years of Political Theory studies in college and grad school and a three-semester course at CVC. Then,

I got a summer Research Grant from the College and wrote the 190-page book in one summer, six hours a day, four days a week. It covers the Classic Thinkers (Plato, Aristotle, Cicero, St. Augustine, Locke, Marx, etc.) and presents them through three categories (Human Nature, Political Society, and Social Ethics) that make it easy to compare thinkers. For example, Aristotle, the ancient Greek philosopher declares, "Man is by nature a Social Animal," by virtue of his human faculties of reasoned speech and moral choice. Marx says humans are "producers" and society is all about economics.

I used this text in my year-long survey class for 30 years and was pleased with how many students liked it because it was simple and clear. It also had extensive quotations from the original writers, which added credibility and objectivity.

My first really scholarly book was *The Political Philosophy of Thomas Jefferson* (Johns Hopkins University Press, 1991) a revision of my Rutgers University doctoral (Ph.D.) dissertation. That took eight years and about 100 rejection slips before it was published beautifully by Johns Hopkins, the oldest university press in America. It became a kind of classic on the subject internationally: the main text of the Jefferson Symposium at Oxford University; the first American book on this Founder to be translated into Russian and published in Moscow, right after the fall of the Soviet Union. This year is the 30th Anniversary of its publication and Johns Hopkins Press is planning to celebrate it.

There followed books on *Religion and Politics*, an anthology of major theologians (St. Augustine, Aquinas, Luther, Calvin, etc.) on politics, and an *Encyclopedia of Political Thought,* most entries of which I wrote, again in one summer (and my daughter claimed I began talking like an encyclopedia at the dinner table!); *The Political Philosophy of James Madison* on the "Father of the United States Constitution"; a popular book on *What Would Jefferson Say?* about contemporary issues; and other co-edited books. Once you established a reputation in a scholarly field you were called upon to contribute book chapters, journal articles, conference papers, and book reviews on that field, of which I did many.

At that time, an academic was to "cut one's teeth" or "prove oneself" in serious scholarship before going on to "light" writing: "Thought Pieces" and "political journalism."

A "Thought Piece" was scholarly in having references and academic themes, but it didn't cite "all the literature" or remain completely objective. My piece on "Constituting the Constitution" for *The Harvard Journal of Law and Public Policy* came out of my lectures on the British Constitution at Oxford University and was such a "Thought Piece". My article on "Burke's Catholic Conservatism" in *Modern Age* was also such a piece, coming out of my research at Trinity College, Dublin. Each, in a way, is more original and important than my strictly scholarly works, and the previous "hard scholarship" lent them credibility. But to do such "soft" scholarship, (such thought "fluff") before serious scholarship was considered inappropriate and unprofessional.

Even worse would be my recent political blog articles (for *AMERICAN GREATNESS* and *GENZ Conservative*) that apply my political theory knowledge to contemporary politics.

Now, unless I feel "led" I plan to suspend writing; focus on videotaping some lectures on Political Theory, Theology, and Law; and enjoy my last years in contemplation.

TRAVELS

Oxford, England

I remember the scene that first morning, looking out the turret window of my rooms at Trinity College, Oxford. It was like a medieval fantasy: stone Gothic college architecture, through the mist, manicured garden beyond, the bells of a dozen college chapels ringing. It seemed like another world–magical.

Oxford, "The City of Dreaming Spires", almost always makes that impression on people: other-worldly, timeless.

As the oldest university in the English-speaking world, beginning in the 12th century with a few small "colleges" (Merton College and St. Edmund's Hall being the first) made up of a priest or monk and a few students, Oxford remains the "Mecca" of Western academia. All with walled-in-confines, center gardens, or "Quads", glorious architecture, steeples, and bells. An air of peace and centuries of intellectual, religious, and political history pervade it. Almost every major event and person in English history has an association with this university city. Now, almost 40 small colleges make up Oxford University. "The "largest" (Christ Church University) might have 500 students. The tutorial system of education still exists there (along with large university lectures): a single Don or tutor meeting with a single, or at most three students to discuss a topic, reading, paper writing, in Socratic style, questioning, discussion, conversation, learning the subject, and more importantly, how to think, examine, contrast, answer, speculate. A scene in the movie *Shadowlands* about C.S. Lewis at Magdalen College, Oxford, with three "readers" during a tutorial displays this world.

I've been in Oxford perhaps a dozen times in the last 30 years, as a lecturer, researcher, visitor, and "Member of Hall". One funny thing about the old English universities is the variety of positions there, all rather indistinct.

At an American university, based on the German model, you have, basically, two types of people: Teachers and Students.

At Oxford, you have:

Professors	Scholars
Tutors	Visitors
Fellows	Leavers
Lecturers	Teachers
Readers	Members

The "leavers" are what we would call "Seniors" or "graduates", (because they are "Leaving". And, after you "Leave" you don't become an "Alum"-- you become an "Old Member" (of Hall or College). I was "in residence" and "commissioned" by Wycliff Hall, (something between graduation and ordination) and now I am an "Old Member".

My adventures at this citadel of academe began in 1991, when an administrator from the University of Virginia, in Charlottesville visited my branch campus in Wise and gave me the name of someone there who wanted to speak to me. I went back to my office and called the number of "Tom Dowd", Senior Director of Program Development, UVA Division of Continuing Education. The phone rang a couple of times and then a loud voice said, "YEA!" Quite puzzled, I replied, "Ah, I'm trying to reach Mr. Thomas Dowd". "WELLLL", the voice intoned, "This is your lucky day! "Ah", I muttered, "is this Mr. Dowd?" "You got him", said the voice.

This exchange began not only my first visit to Oxford but a now 30-year friendship with one of the funniest, brightest, and best people in the world.

He had come across my just-released book, The Political Philosophy of Thomas Jefferson, in the UVA bookstore and wanted me to speak at the "Jefferson Symposium on the Lawn" in the summer of 1992. This was an annual event that brought mostly UVA Alumni (not Leavers) back to their beloved Charlottesville and "Mr. Jefferson's University" for a week of study, tours, dinners, and events. I was honored to be involved.

But then, Tom Down, President Casteen, and others at the University and Oxford developed a conference idea: *Exploring the English Origins of Mr. Jefferson's Political Thought* at Trinity

College, a 16th-century institution in the "old" section on Broad Street next to *Balliol* and *The Sheldonian*.

I was thrilled to teach at this program and have my book on Jefferson be the symposium text. It was a "Dream Come True" for any American academy, and at 40, early in my career.

I will never forget the opening tea and reception in the Hall of Trinity College. I was admiring a teacup and saucer with the college crest on it and remarked," This is nice, I'd like to steal one."

At that moment someone nudged me and said, "I'd like to introduce you to David Eastwood, Senior Tutor at Pembroke College, who will be leading the English side of the Symposium.

A man about my age shook my hand. "Oh dear," I said, "an official of Oxford University and I am talking about stealing cups!" He smiled and replied, "Ah, but not an official of Trinity College." We became fast friends. Similar in attitude, and scholarly interests in 18th-century British and American political thought, we also both enjoyed a good joke. He asked me, "Are we to have the 'Sheldonian' Jefferson at the conference?"

I replied, "Sheldonian?" Er, no that's down the street from here". (Referring to the Sheldonian Theatre or university auditorium on Broad Street, built by my ancestor Gilbert Sheldon, Restoration Archbishop of Canterbury, after being chancellor of Oxford, and Master of Trinity College.

When they found that I was related to a prominent Member of the College, they showed me an oil portrait of him in which they claimed to see a family resemblance (which evaded me) and thought he was "more ruddy", whatever that means.

The Oxford Symposium was uneventful, but the life at the College, visiting other colleges and churches, dinner in the Hall, tours of notable historic sites, and all the shops, restaurants, museums, and pubs was fascinating. But, the greatest treat of my first visit to Oxford was the English people, characters, and experiences created before by some of my favorite writers: P.G. Wodehouse, Evelyn Waugh, Osbert Lancaster, and Sir John Mortimer.

An old Oxford College is surrounded by a high wall, entered through a locked "gate" upon which you enter a "lodge" where the "porter" lives to attend guests. The "rooms" are off a "staircase" usually consisting of a sitting room with a fireplace, couch, chair, bookcases, and tables, adjoined by a small room with a bed, a wardrobe, and a sink with a mirror. A "scout" or servant attends to the room and its residents. I'll never forget shaving in the sink, looking up at the mirror, and seeing a thin elderly man behind me holding a very ragged small towel. When I caught his eye he said, "Fresh towel, then?" I took it from my Scout, thanked him, and handed him my equally thin, soaked towel, grateful to get a dry one.

At Trinity College, Oxford, at this time the Scouts were an elderly couple. The wife attended the girls in the college. One of the symposium members, a middle-aged American woman, woke up one morning to see her Scout staring down in her face. After saying "Good Morning", the Scout inquired, "Where is your husband'?"

The guest said, "Oh, he's probably gone out for an early jog." The old servant replied, "Why, is he impotent?" (meaning in England: weak, sickly, or frail).

At one point during our week-long symposium at Oxford, a high official from UVA visited. In the evenings, I often took a walk, admiring the setting sunlight on the glowing light sandstone of the buildings. This evening, I ran into this official going out also, so we walked together. He pointed out various sites, colleges, and institutes, where he had spoken, received honors, and been given degrees.

I talked about the weather. It had been an unusually cold summer, even for England. My wife, Elaine, before I had departed made me two nightshirts: one light cotton for warm weather, and one heavy flannel for cold. I'd worn the warm wool one the whole time! I mentioned this to the official. He stopped in his tracks and stared at me, wide-eyed. "Your wife MAKES you things?"! A bit embarrassed by his response, I mumbled "Well, er, yes, ah, occasionally". His eyes got even wider, as he gazed upwards, whispering, "If I ever asked my wife to make me something..." Then he shuttered, trembled, shook himself, and we walked on.

Besides the close lifelong friendships formed that summer at Oxford with (now) Sir David Eastwood, Tom Dowd, and others, I enjoyed experiencing the talk and manners of the English. When one jostled with someone on the often-crowded sidewalks, they would not say, "Excuse me," but rather, "Sorry". This was heard dozens of times on any walk. And despite the historic reserve of the British, I found many to be extremely kind and friendly.

A few years later I spent a Sabbatical Leave at Wycliffe Hall, Oxford, then Headed by the famous English Theologian Alistar McGrath, during Trinity Term.

WYCLIFFE HALL

Besides chapel services, visiting seminars, and tutors, I did research on 14th-century English Political and Religious thought. Research at the college and university libraries, known as the Bodleian or "Bod", interviewing Oxford scholars in the field, invariably involving being invited to Hall for lunch and the senior common room for tea. I found the academics uniformly hospitable, polite, and helpful. Clearly "academic courtesy" was a part of their creed.

My family, wife Elaine, and two young children accompanied me to Oxford, where we lived for almost three months in a large apartment in North Oxford. We would all join the students and staff for lunch in the Hall dining room, getting to know many people very well. One student couple, also with young children, took us all to a nearby zoo.

My wife took the kids to London, St. Paul's Cathedral, Blenheim Palace, and "May Day", and we all took the rail to the Midlands of Northern England, to see the area from where my family descended near Derbyshire and Bakewell. I honestly thought I noticed a family resemblance to the people there!

But I also experienced the notorious British "snub" or "cutting". This is the famous, especially upper-class, "ignoring of their inferiors". We'd had a nobleman speak to our group after dinner one night in the Hall, giving a very good and gracious talk, especially about Anglo-American relations, and our shared Christian heritage.

The Lord was sitting across the table from me, so when he sat down, I leaned over and complimented him on his speech. No reply! Not even a look or acknowledgment of my remarks or even my existence. So, I thought he must not have heard me. I said it louder and louder. Finally, in unfeigned disgust, he glanced at me, smiled weakly, and nodded. Clearly, I was beneath talking to, or perhaps I'd violated the old rule that you can only speak with people seated next to you.

Later, I realized it was the classic English "snub" that I had read about in British novels and seen on British TV programs. It does, indeed, "cut one to the quick".

A few years after my first visit to Oxford I was at a religious conference and at dinner, the subject of England came up. A minister seated near me asked if I knew of Wycliffe Hall, the Evangelical Anglican College at Oxford. I didn't. He spoke highly of it, especially of its principal and headmaster and president, Alistair McGrath, a very prominent English theologian.

I had gotten my endowed chair by then and had my first sabbatical leave coming up, so I emailed Dr. McGrath and he responded warmly and hospitably, welcoming me to join the Hall as an Academic Visitor for the Trinity Term 2002.

Wycliffe Hall was a relatively new Oxford College (late 1800s) with about 100 graduate theological students destined to become priests in the Church of England. At that time it was a close, lively academic and social community with a wonderful Christian spirit.

In the Midlands, my daughter and I took a bus circuit around the area past the village of Sheldon. When I mentioned to the local tourist office that I wanted to see the old family grounds, she said, "Oh you don't want to go THERE". It wasn't high on the tourist sites, being a tiny village of a church, a school, a pub, an inn, and a few modest houses.

The landscape of the Midlands, as I mentioned earlier, was identical to the Southwest Virginia mountains I settled with rugged hills, broad valleys, and rivers. Some genetic memory must have been at work here.

Wycliffe Hall is situated in the "newer" section of the university near "the parks" and the cricket field. A few hodgepodge gothic and Victorian buildings make up the small and humble college.

Rev. McGrath graciously asked me if I wished to be included in the "Commissioning Ceremony" at the end of the year at the nearby church. I was honored. To be "Commissioned" was sort of halfway between graduation and ordination, another vague British academic practice.

I have kept in contact with my "old college" ever since, visiting regularly, and serving on a United States Alumni Board. After McGrath left for a position in London, the Hall went through some rough times (as all colleges do) with controversy and falling enrollment. But a few years ago, a new Principal, Reverend Michael Lloyd helped restore the Hall in spirit and academic quality. Today, it is a healthy Christian institution in Oxford. Principal Lloyd's humor, wisdom, and love of Handel's sacred music made a quick bond between us.

Hertford College, Oxford

Most summers from 2004 to 2011 I taught a course on "English and American Constitutionalism" at one of the oldest colleges, Hertford, properly pronounced "Hartford", like my old grammar school. It sat right at the center of Oxford, across from the Sheldonian Theatre and Bodleian Library. Many famous "alums" went there, including Thomas Hobbs and Evelyn Waugh. The course was a Regent University (Virginia) graduate course, primarily for their Law School and Government students. My good friend and colleague Jeffry Morrison (now at Christopher Newport University) led it and taught the "American" side. I taught the first half on the subject of the English constitution (of which I had only a passing acquaintance). My old Oxford friend David Eastwood advised me on texts, including the classic *The English Constitution* by Walter Bagehot. I also found a book of English political documents of the 17th century, which was very useful, as most all of British constitutional history is summarized in the 1600's from the Absolute Monarchy of Charles I to the Radical Democracy of Cromwell's Puritan Commonwealth, to the "mixed" constitution of today: Monarchy, Lords, and Commons, or "The King in Parliament."

We had about twenty students, mostly from Regent, but others from around the world (especially Africa and Latin America).

We lived in Hertford residence halls in South Oxford. As a Christian university, it involved morning prayers together after breakfast, various social events, and a glorious final dinner in the ancient Hertford College Hall. It was a close, fun group. I recall the farewell party involving gifts, cards, and watching *Mr. Bean* videos.

I learned in the course of this course that the famous "unwritten" British constitution was really a "Cultural constitution" – including government, laws, religion, family, education, etc. I wrote an essay for *The Harvard Journal of Law* on "Constituting the Constitution: Understanding the American Constitution Through the Traditional British Constitution". It showed the cultural constitution in the U.S.A. through Alex de Tocqueville's famous book *Democracy in America.*

Before discovering this, I asked several British academic, governmental, and Church officials what the British Constitution was. They uniformly answered, "Well, it is not like the American; I mean, it isn't a single written document, rather it's uh, er well...ah, WELL we really don't know what it is, do we?"

Every one of the 40 Oxford Colleges has a "college tie". I bought a Hertford tie (with a Hart or Deer on it). Years before I had tried to buy a Wycliffe Hall tie as an Oxford shop owner said, "Wycliffe Hall?" NO! He explained that he had to buy ties in lots of 50. "Do you know how long it would take for me to sell 50 Wycliffe Hall ties?! Finally, the Hall brought out its own tie, with crosses of white on a dark blue background.

My last visit to Oxford was to present a paper on Political Theology at a conference at the University Church: St. Mary the Virgin. This was held in a tiny ancient room that had been the original library when the University consisted of a few small medieval colleges. This was in December 2015. I haven't been back since, but I hope someday to return to "The City of Dreaming Spires".

Istanbul, Turkey

My view of the old city of Istanbul from the window of the 10th-floor hotel room was extraordinary. All gray stucco buildings with red tile roofs, the sun shimmering on the Bosphorus Channel beyond Minarets of large mosques shooting high up to the sky. The most exotic place I'd ever seen.

The ancient city, originally Constantinople, the capital of the Eastern Roman Empire, named for Emperor Constantine who made Christianity the official religion of the empire, became the capital of the Moslem Ottoman Empire. After World War I, this Empire was divided up, leaving only the nation of Turkey, with this still cosmopolitan capital. But now, a modern "Western" Republic formed under the reformist leader Kemal Ataturk.

I first went there in the mid-1990s as an ambassador (with Provost George Culbertson) from my college, making an exchange agreement with a Turkish university. This began, as another colleague, Vice Chancellor for Development, Brent Kennedy wrote a book on the Melungeons, a native population ostensibly descended from Turks who landed in America before the Spanish.

The leading British scholar of the Constitution in England was Vernon Bogdanor of Brasenose College, Oxford, who spoke to our class. He also had me for sherry in his rooms and gave the best description possible of their constitution. I asked what the British people thought of their constitution or matters like religious freedom, democracy, the right to bear arms, etc. He replied, "They aren't AMERICANS! Most don't think about it much", or words to that effect.

His college was named after a brass door knocker on the "gate" of the original medieval school shaped like a lion's face, hence, "brass nose". One of the most distinguished colleges at Oxford is named for a door knocker.

One memorable incident in the class on the "organic" social constitution was when I was describing it and a woman student from Latin America began weeping. (This is not unusual. I often have had women come into my class, burst into tears, and run out of the room). But this was a kind of muffled, quiet sobbing. Finally, I asked if anything was wrong. She said I was describing her country with traditions, customs, and history, that the current socialist state was systematically destroying.

Our class also worshiped in various Oxford churches: St. Aldates, the "student" Anglican Church; Christ Church Cathedral; and St Mary Magdalene, the "high church", Oxford Movement, Anglo-Catholic Church.

Years later at my retirement roast, Commonwealth Attorney Chuck Slemp recalled the beautiful choral music at Evensong in the Cathedral.

Besides these experiences in Oxford, I was able to make some side trips during my time there. A memorable one was to one of my favorite writers, Sir John Mortimer, and his farmhouse in Oxfordshire near Henley. It was a complicated train ride to that town and when I finally arrived all the taxi cabs were off for lunch. At last, one took me to Mortimer's house where he entertained me graciously. He had written the popular *Rumpole of the Bailey* series and had adapted Evelyn Waugh's *Brideshead Revisited* for film.

I also loved the Turkish tea, very strong but served in tiny glasses too hot to hold in an untrained hand. At every government office I visited, I was given such tea, with cakes, which made the visit very pleasant. I met with an official of the President's Office; a Supreme Court Justice. Various university officials and professors; including a General in their "Pentagon"; were all very helpful in my research on modern Turkey and its Founder, Ataturk.

A funny thing kept happening I was mistaken for a Turk and my guide/interpreter was the "American". The mistake was an honest one. He was of Macedonian heritage: fair and blond. I saw soon that I resembled Turkish people in features (square), color (medium brown), and even blue eyes. Often, we'd enter an office, and someone would start talking to me in Turkish. My guide would shout, "I'm the Turk! HE'S the American.!" The physical cause of that amusing error was discovered years later when I did the Ancestry DNA testing and found I had 7% West Asian (Turkey, Iberian Peninsula, Northwestern Middle East). Perhaps one of my ancestors brought back a souvenir from the Crusade!

At university, I met privately with a group of professors who expressed concern over the country's drift from a "secular" Western Republic (with freedom of speech and religion) to an Islamic State resembling Middle Eastern Arab Countries. A religious revival was clearly occurring, with new mosques being built all over. All I could offer was the Jeffersonian belief that freedom of religion pleases God (or Allah) as He is not impressed by people coerced to be among the Faithful.

I haven't kept up with Turkish politics since the 1990s but I believe it has moved in the direction they feared.

At the "Pentagon" in Ankara, I met with a top general. Walking down the long hallway to his office, the Turkish soldiers standing guard at each door, on a platform, at attention, helmets in line with their noses, bayoneted rifles at their sides: it was a frightening sight.

The Turkish Army is known for its fierceness and this view confirmed it. That is how they managed to remain neutral during WWII.

Turkish authorities took an interest in this early link with the USA and Brent Kennedy had visited there frequently. A proposed trip was prevented by another obligation, and he asked me to fill in for him.

In Turkey, I spoke with several governmental, academic, and business representatives. Almost all boast of their founder Ataturk and his reforms in politics, religion, education, and economics. His emphasis on democracy, freedom, and independence increasingly reminded me of my hero, Thomas Jefferson, and I mentioned this to a few.

When I returned home, Brent told me the Government of Turkey would support my writing of a book comparing Jefferson and Ataturk. This was completed a few years later as *Jefferson and Ataturk: Political Philosophies*.

But this required another trip to Turkey for research on Ataturk involving interviews with governmental, judicial, military, academic, business, and religious leaders. Things have changed dramatically in that country since then, but I had some extraordinary experiences in Turkey in the 1990s.

I was immediately struck by the exotic scenery of Istanbul and the wonderful hospitality of the Turkish people. I seemed to be an honored American guest and toured many sites of the old Ottoman Empire, including the Sultan's Palace and the main room made up mostly of cushions all around the floor.

Enormous and elaborate meals were served to me. I've always liked Mediterranean food, especially Greek lamb, rice, and spices, but I found Turkish cuisine even better. At one luncheon at an outdoor restaurant on the Bosphorus Channel, I was asked what kind of food I especially liked. It told them about lamb, wild rice, and spices. The waiter said they had six side dishes and would bring out a "sample" of each so I could decide which I liked best. These "samples" were full-sized meals and after "tasting" them I was too full to order my "favorite".

At another evening banquet, I was served so many dishes that I was stuffed by dessert time and could not eat another bite, greatly offending the hostess.

At this time, Turkey was a "secular" Moslem republic. This meant it was overwhelmingly Islamic culturally, but it was not an official part of the state, and tolerance was enjoyed by Christians, Jews, Hindus, and other religious minorities.

One of the most impressive sights I've ever seen was in downtown Istanbul at noon on Friday, the Moslem Holy Day. As the Call to Prayer resonated from a dozen mosques, the crowded streets emptied–everyone flowing into the mosque to pray, their overflowing to the surrounding lot, street, everywhere. All standing, bowing, kneeling, prostrating themselves, eyes closed, trembling, crying, grimacing. I asked my guide what the devout were thinking. He said, "They feel they are standing before Allah!"

One Saturday I experienced this more personally. I found myself in the study of the Imam (religious head) of the Blue Mosque–the Holiest Moslem Shrine in the Ottoman Empire. This visit was not on the itinerary and the Iman, a gentle-looking old man, seemed as confused as I felt being there. The Moslem terrorism that swept the world a few years later had not occurred, but several Moslem terrorist attacks had occurred in Israel and some European countries. At any rate, it was an awkward situation. I didn't know what this leader's view on The Infidel was and felt concerned after having read the Koran and spoken with some American Muslims.

My interpreter asked me what I wanted to say to the Imam. I felt strange and afraid. All I could do was silently pray and ask the Lord's guidance. I asked myself, "What Would Jesus Do?"

Then I turned to the interpreter and said, "Please tell the Iman that I am an American and a Christian and I just want to apologize to him and his people for any evil or cruelty we have done them and to assure him that any hateful acts were not in the Spirit of Christ". The interpreter stared wide-eyed at me. "I can't say THAT to the Imam; I am a Turk and a Muslim!"

"Go ahead," I said. He spoke my word. The Imam sat silently staring at the floor for about two minutes. Then he spoke to the interpreter who said to me. "The Imam says that the Koran says that the greatest thing a man can do is speak the truth." We then smiled at each other and our 30-minute scheduled meeting lasted two hours, discussing theology, history, and prayer. Afterward, he took me into the "Holy of Holies" of the Blue Mosque where only clerics could pray. He gave me his prayer beads.

I gave him a small brass vial with scented anointing oil in it. He sniffed it and said he would hang it on the wall of his study there.

Another miracle occurred the following Sunday. I was looking for a church near my hotel and set off for the 11:00 Service. I came upon one; it was Greek Orthodox. Two men stood guard at the entrance blocking me. They asked who I was and what I wanted. I said I was an American and a Christian and would like to attend their church service. One looked at me suspiciously. "You're not Catholic, are you?!

"No", I assured him. "Just Christian" (I didn't think he'd know what a Baptist was.) They reluctantly led me into the small sanctuary, empty but for a bearded old priest and a few old women lighting candles. I prayed silently for a few minutes and left.

There was a Church of England (Anglican) parish on this street, and I walked up and down but never saw it. Finally, I asked a policeman/soldier standing on guard if he knew where it was. He answered "No", but directed me to the British Embassy nearby. They answered the door and directed me to the church which was on the street but way back and down, not visible. By now it was late, to see people entering the building. It turned out it was the end of daylight-saving time, that day (unbeknownst to me) and so we gained an hour as clocks were set back and it was 11:00 instead of noon, just in time for worship!

Since I'd grown up with it, it was a joy to experience the *Book of Common Prayer* in this distant land. At the typical "coffee hour" socializing after service, I spoke with the priest and several English people, including one from Oxford!

One other funny thing I remember about my visit to Turkey was the university students (all boys) who served as my guides around their schools. They were very interested in the U.S. asking all about America, our society, education, economy, and my life. When I told them about my work family home, friends, cars, land, animals, and social life, they exclaimed, "He lives like a Traditional Turkish Man!!!"

I returned home and wrote the book on *Jefferson and Ataturk: Political Philosophies,* published by my old press, Peter Lang, and still in print today.

I have not returned to Istanbul again, and Turkey has changed greatly, but I am privileged to have visited that fascinating and beautiful place.

Moscow, Russia

As the airline descended into Moscow airport that November morning, I was surprised to see how desolate the countryside was around that Russian capital. Bare fields, broken twisted fences, ramshackle houses, and scrubby landscape. I had expected the area around the major city of one of the most powerful countries in the world to be more impressive in appearance.

I had been invited to visit Russia because a professor at Moscow State University was translating my book, The Political Philosophy of Thomas Jefferson, for publication in his country with support from the United States Information Agency (U.S.I.A). I was told it was the first American book on Jefferson to be printed in the former U.S.S.R. I had a letter from Nikita P., who had been a leading Soviet scholar on Jefferson, to assist with the translation and he could only communicate via the new "email" as regular mail and international phone calls were too expensive. Remember, this was before the Internet! I was the first faculty member at the college to get a computer and email, just to do this project.

At the Russian publication of PPTJ, I was invited to a reception at the Moscow publisher and asked to speak at a conference on emerging Russian democracy.

When I arrived at the Moscow airport I was approached by the driver to take me to my lodgings. I was rescued just in time by Prof. P. who told me that this was a common scam, where I would have been robbed, stripped, and left in the countryside to freeze to death.

My government apartment had a kitchen, and we went to buy food from a store that had few items. The meat server and clerk were two difficult people, as someone told me later "The Communists" kept you healthy until they shipped you off to Siberia"

The first evening a young woman appeared, A Canadian professor for the conference; but after seeing we were alone, she left for other lodgings. That's how I know I was under surveillance–as the next day my host said, "What was a woman doing in your room last night?!

It was bitterly cold in Russia in November and the whole atmosphere was cold, dark, and depressed. I longed for warm friendly Istanbul!

At the conference, mostly Soviet scholars spoke, always denouncing the U.S. and Gorbachev (who ended Communism). I finally turned to my guide and said, "This is kind of anti-American". He said, "Oh, don't worry, these are the Moderates!"

It was the most unstructured meeting I had ever seen; no program or schedule, just the leader calling on participants randomly. There was one other American of notably unimpressive appearance, the Canadian woman, and a British Marxist.

When I was called on to give my paper, it was on Early American Democracy and what Russia might benefit from knowing about it. I opened with a Russian fable I'd gotten from a Literature professor and ended with Old Testament Scripture:

> If my people who are called by my name
> Will humble themselves and pray and seek
> My Face, and turn from their wicked ways,
> Then I will hear from heaven and will forgive
> Their sins and heal their land.
> *2 Chronicles 7:14*

When I ended my talk the conference head said, "We began with a fable and ended with the Bible." But there was an almost reverent silence during the reading of the Scripture by my translator.

The post-Soviet economy was extremely poor. I recall an old Russian woman sitting in the Moscow subway selling one little bottle of shampoo. At a conference break, they had a table of food and drinks including a plate with small Cadbury chocolate bars. As I surveyed the offerings, a small hand poked through the crowd, snatched up all the bars, and pulled back. I looked and it was an old Russian scholar smirking as he stuffed the booty into his pockets.

Despite the widespread hatred of change, many Russians told me that even with guaranteed housing, health care, and employment (and constant police state surveillance and control) almost everyone was willing to risk poverty to get some freedom. However, my host had mixed feelings about the influx of capitalism. Walking down a busy street in the city, he pointed at ads for ladies' lingerie, and said, "Is that decent?!"

Almost all the old former Communist academics were Directors of some "Institute" proudly displayed on their business cards.

I lectured on Political Theory in a class at Moscow University. The students looked like students everywhere: talking, laughing, flirting. After my summary of the "Western Political Thought", so different from their Marxist indoctrination, one young man asked me, "Since we Russians messed up the Republic and Socialism, do you think we should go back to the Czar?"

Fortunately, my Midwest decorum and academic professionalism kept me from bursting out laughing. I said, "Well, of course, that is up to Russians, but the Czars were part of a whole system (economic, religious, social) that may be impossible to restore".

They proudly showed me the library atop the "Wedding Cake" main building of Moscow State University. I asked in the reference section if there were any American academic journals. They showed me a shelf of the American Political Science Review, our leading journal. As I looked through one, I noticed half the articles were cut out – Censored.

The conference ended with a large banquet and endless late-night toasts. At one point, the Head sent a man down to me saying, "The Director wants the American to give a toast. I rose, raised my glass nervously, and said thanks for the conference; hope for future peaceful relations between our countries; and appreciation for this opportunity. As I sat down the Canadian professor, who spoke Russian, whispered to me, "You blew them away! They didn't expect a gracious toast from the monstrous Americans."

I found in Russia, as in other countries, a mixture of hatred, respect, and fear of America. One official told me whenever they faced a difficult policy question someone would finally say, "How do the Americans do it?"

Before I left Russia (a visit of about two weeks) a group of us were taken to a small village north of Moscow. It consisted of eight small cottages, four on each side of a dirt road, a common barn, and a dairy. Each house had a small backyard, full of potatoes, and a great pile of firewood. We were served a dinner of fresh potatoes with fresh creamery butter (delicious – I ate three helpings, much to the aged woman "babushka" hostess's delight). On the hearth above the enormous fireplace was a Russian Orthodox Church icon (picture) of the Blessed Virgin Mary holding the Baby Jesus, behind two tall candles. I thought, "Where are the Communists?" Eighty years of official atheism had not wiped out Russian religion and spirituality. My later studies of Edmund Burke and Political Culture confirmed that a country's culture, traditions, and values change very slowly, indeed.

Before I left Russia, I tried to convert my remaining rubles back to American dollars. The bank clerk informed me that they did not have enough currency to make the exchange. My companion, Professor P. stared at her and said in a loud voice, "It's a BANK!" She went back and returned with my dollars.

The next year, I arranged for my Russian host to visit Virginia; have a fellowship at Monticello; and speak at my College. He remarked that American students were so informal, "They just come up and speak to their professors!" With one day left of his visit and no appointments, I asked him if there was anything he'd like to see, any place he'd like to visit. He shouted, "WAL-MART!!!"

I took him to our small local store where he wandered about gazing in wonder at all the goods we took for granted. He bought a case of dishwasher soap. Russia had dishwashers but no soap. At the check-out, he asked about a fluid for keeping rain off windshields and asked if I thought he should buy some. I replied that he might if he thought it would help his car. "I don't have a car," he said. I suggested that if he didn't own a car, it might not be of use to him. He bought it anyway.

I kept in touch with Nikita for a few years, but then communication slowed down and finally ceased. Last I heard, his exalted position as a Professor under Soviet Communism was reduced to teaching many classes for low fees at multiple schools around Moscow. I recommended to a missionary going to Russia to look him up, but when he tried, he informed me that "Nikita P" was not his real name; it was one of many aliases -- this one reserved for Americans.

Later, I heard that there was little interest in my book on Jefferson in Russia and the remainder were packed up and shipped to Belarus.

I found Russia to have all the sadness, darkness, sentimentality, and depression common in Russian Literature. It may be the cold climate and historic tragedies and cruelties. In any event, I found it both repelling and appealing and have no desire to return.

Vienna, Austria

Vienna, Austria is the most beautiful city on earth. Imperial Capital of the Hapsburg (Austrian-Hungarian) Empire which ruled Central and Eastern Europe for 700 years, is a piece of art. Around "The Ring" – a boulevard that circles the Old City are the Classical, Gothic, and Baroque buildings of the Royal Palace, the Opera House, the Parliament, the Cathedral, and the University. Around these masterpieces are gardens, statues, fountains, and other gorgeous buildings.

It was also special to me as the home of my favorite Classical music composers: Mozart and Haydn. Attending mass at Peterskirke (St. Peter's Church) also introduced to me what is now my favorite music: Classical Sacred. We all know a few such pieces: Handel's *Messiah*; Mozart's *Requiem*; Vivaldi's *Gloria*; but I wasn't aware of the enormous volume of Sacred or Christian church music by these Classical 18th Century composers. They now are an enormous collection I enjoy at home, in the car, and in the bath. The combination of the beautiful, lively Classical music with religious choir themes is my favorite now.

I learned this by attending sung mass at Peterskirke on a side street down from St. Stephen's Cathedral. The services there were spoken in Latin and German, but mostly sung. I recall, besides the Catholic ritual, an old priest preaching in German with such evangelical fervor it brought tears to my eyes, even though I only understood the occasional word.

My first trip to Vienna around 2004 began with an email from a professor at the University asking me to review his book manuscript on Jefferson, having read my *The Political Philosophy of Thomas Jefferson*. George C. was about my age, interested in Political Theory, and very humorous.

This led to an invitation to give a lecture in one of his classes at the University of Vienna. I recall the quaint custom of the Austrian students of applauding by knocking their knuckles on their desks.

While there, I met the Head of the Department of Political Science (or "Institut Für Politikwissenschaft"). She welcomed me to teach a class on American Political Thought during my upcoming Sabbatical in 2007. That occurred during their spring/summer term and was mostly made up of Austrian students with a mix of other E.U. countries, as well as a group of conservative Moslem women from Turkey (in burkas), and an Australian. All spoke English.

I recall one young lady in the class, from Austria, tall and aristocratic-looking, but compulsive in asking questions after almost every sentence of my lectures. Once, during a lecture on the U.S. Constitution's First Amendment guarantee of Freedom of Speech, a young man from Russia raised his hand and asked, "Professor, does the Freedom of Speech include asking interminable stupid questions?" The class broke out in laughter; the girl turned red; and I tried to tactfully answer that (as with

Freedom of Press) we often had to take the rough with the smooth.

Another day, I was to lecture, as announced, on Freedom of Religion, after our lunch break. As I began the lecture, I noticed all the Turkish Muslim women missing, probably forbidden to attend. Then, as I passed the partly open door, I saw them huddled in the hallway, listening intently.

On my first, exploratory visit to Vienna, I stayed at an 18th Century hotel just across the Danube from the Old City. Beautiful paintings of palace balls and Austrian countryside adorned the room of the quaint inn named for a Hapsburg princess. Walking out the front door one morning I noticed an old church next door and a plaque noting that Joseph Haydn had been Chapelmeister there. I almost fainted (as I did later, passing a house near Stephensplatz with a plaque announcing Mozart had lived there). It was like a Catholic going to Rome, or a Moslem to Mecca (or an academic to Oxford). Holy Ground!

Austria was very clean, neat, and orderly. Polite. Beautiful. But not particularly friendly. I hardly spoke with any of my colleagues at the University. I suspect that I was viewed there (as in Russia and Turkey) as possibly American C.I.A. Any U.S. official, journalist, or academic is suspected of this, which in my case was unjustified.

I recall a Fulbright Fellow from Mexico at my Virginia College telling me casually, "You are C.I.A."

I said, "What makes you think that?"

He replied, "You LOOK like C.I.A.!"

I assured him that I was merely a professor at an obscure little College and pastor of a small church. He smiled and said, "Those are the best COVERS!"

My family spent part of the two months in Vienna with me, in a large apartment within walking distance of the University. We enjoyed performances at the Opera House; visiting historic sights and parks, and traveling to Salzburg.

Once, when walking home from the University, right across from the Opera House, a man came up to me and asked something in German. As always, I said, "Sprechen ze Englishe?"

He replied in English with a strong German accent, "Can you tell me where the Opera House is?" I pointed across the street.

One of my favorite "haunts" was the outdoor café across from St. Stephen's Cathedral (the big open plaza called Stephensplatz), drinking tea and watching the sights. Often, as in the movie *Amadeus*, about Mozart, street performers (mimes, jugglers, etc.) amused us. Once, a rather strange-looking man sitting next to me inhaled with pleasure the smoke from my cigar. We got to talking and he pointed at the Cathedral, saying, "God is not in there!" I visited that Cathedral once as a tourist and was impressed that midday mass was being conducted and tourists blocked off.

As I left Vienna, the plane flew past the snow-capped Alps and above the beautiful rolling, green Austrian countryside and I felt so grateful to have been there.

Israel

About ten years ago, a member of my church, Bobby Tuck, was invited to visit Israel under the auspices of AIPAC (American–Israel Public Affairs Committee) and asked to suggest others, including me.

AIPAC involves strengthening relations (political, military, economic, social) between Israel and the U.S. As an Evangelical Christian who understands the Bible at a literal as well as a metaphorical level, I believed God's statement to Abraham and His People Israel (Genesis 12:3). "I will bless those who bless you and curse those who curse you." as a truth. Despite theological differences, I consider Jews as St. Paul did, God's original Chosen People, never forsaken, and to be honored. I sensed that "Chosen" meant "ideal" or truest humans – with all the human abilities and foibles exemplified in this race. The greatest reverence with the greatest worldliness, highest brilliance with the greatest distraction, (Marx, Freud, etc.) most energy, humor, sociability, passion, hatred of any race. I've only found one characteristic missing from the many Hebrews I've encountered: boredom. Young, old, rich, poor, educated, ignorant, from any country, I've never met a boring Jew. They've all been interesting.

And I believe God has blessed America because of our (relatively) good treatment of that population (legally, if not always culturally).

Educated in New York and New Jersey, I came to know many Jewish people and looked forward to visiting Israel.

It was a weeklong whirlwind tour. A group of perhaps twenty Evangelical American Christians rose early and rushed through a day of tours, meals, visits to religious sites, meetings with government and academic heads, and artistic and musical performances, traversing this tiny country in an elaborate luxurious bus. Exhausting but rewarding.

I witnessed the holy sites familiar in the Bible: The Temple in Jerusalem; the Garden of Gethsemani; the Tomb of Jesus; the Mount of Olives; and the site of the Cross. Most awesome to me was Nazareth, Galilee, where Jesus grew up and returned after His Resurrection. We stayed at a Kibbutz near the Sea of Galilee, and I arose very early one morning to sit on the shore as the sun rose over the lake on which Jesus walked, on the beach, perhaps, where He met His disciples after His death. It gave my Faith new depth and wonder.

We shopped for souvenirs where I bought a Jerusalem Cross in rosewood and a cooking utensil for my wife (which the others teased me about).

On the Northern border, we saw Israeli tanks facing off against Arab missiles. In Gaza we *heard* Palestinian missiles being fired into Israel, warning sirens sounding, hiding for cover in nearby shelters, and hearing the explosions terrifying the local population.

One state official we met was head of the Anti-Terrorism Unit and I never saw such a nervous man in my life. Pacing back and forth, chain-smoking cigarettes, jingling coins in his pocket, he described the daily threats of missiles, suicide bombers, Iranian incursions, etc. The whole country was under military alert constantly, the young men and women doing compulsory service in uniforms everywhere.

Despite this historic and warlike atmosphere, some of the newer sections of Jerusalem and Tel Aviv looked almost like an American city: shops, restaurants, crowds.

After returning from Israel, I regularly attended the annual AIPAC Policy Conference in the big Convention Center in Washington, D.C. About 18,000 of God's Chosen People are in that giant facility. Such energy! Much of the activities were academic, presentations, and seminars on politics. It was like a giant university. The Jewish people from all over the world welcomed this "Goy" or Christian minister with warmth and interest. As with the Irish, they would just walk up to you, striking up a conversation, and expressing appreciation for a non-Jew's interest in Judaism and Israel. Brilliant, fast-talking, funny, lively. One thinks of the culture in *Fiddler on the Roof*.

At one banquet I was seated next to a rugged young man who told me he was "the only Jewish tuna importer in Japan". He asked me what I did and when I told him I was a Christian minister, he said, "A CHRISTIAN MINISTER! Oh, no! Now I have to be polite!" My love of the Jewish-American comedians Woody Allen and Larry David helped me relate. At a VIP reception, an attractive young woman noticed my tag saying, "Special Guest". She said, "So, what makes you so 'Special'?" I replied, "I think it's that I'm not Jewish."

Before being introduced to speak to one group, the host asked me my title. I said, "Let's keep it informal: The Reverend Doctor Professor." He laughed.

I attended the spring AIPAC Conference in 2016 where all the Presidential Candidates addressed the Convention (except one of Jewish descent: Bernie Sanders). Soon-to-be President Trump received much applause, despite most attendees being Democrats.

After every AIPAC conference, we would meet with our Congressional representatives about concerns of mutual interest to Israel and America. My Congressman Morgan Griffith was very welcoming and gracious (and well-informed).

I have not kept up much with AIPAC or Israel the past few years, but I will always be appreciative of their bringing me to Israel.

Ireland

It's easy to see why Ireland is called "The Emerald Isle". You see it flying into England (which is a dark green landscape) and it is a bright, light green almost glowing like a jewel. This "Land of Saints and Scholars" is special to me as my mother's "Garrett" family (as well as the Hopkins and Kellogg's on my father's side) hale from this enchanted place. My Mother was "Black Irish" (as opposed to green-eyed, red-haired "Red Irish") with pale white skin, jet black hair, and dark blue eyes. I saw many women in Dublin who resembled my mom in coloring and features. So, I know where I got it from (including making jokes, playing pranks, being called "an imp" by her).

I also saw the resemblance between the Irish and my community in rural Southwestern Virginia – besides physical features, strong ties to family, faith, community, and friendship. The humor and music (Old Time/Bluegrass) are seen in *The Andy Griffith Show*. Most here claimed to be "Scots-Irish" but that was just another trick on the English!

My opportunity to visit The Emerald Isle came during my sabbatical leave to Trinity College, Dublin, when I proposed to study the Anglo-Irish political philosopher Edmund Burke, who attended Trinity in the mid-18th Century and whose papers were in the Archives of The Old Library.

It was 2013 and I was technically In Residence at the Politics Department, but their rather cool reception and distance from the main campus where I lived (along with the Dean, Patrick G., being a Burke Scholar and very welcoming) limited my contact with them.

Burke is a very famous Conservative thinker whose statue adorns the entrance to the College. When I bought some cigars at a tobacconist across from Trinity, the proprietor asked what I was studying. I said, "Edmund Burke; ever heard of him?"

He rose up and loudly proclaimed, "Never!"

My exploratory visit in 2012 found me at an old hotel bordering St. Stephen's Green, near the old Dublin Main Street and Trinity: a beautiful large green park where I often walked. On leave, I lived in college housing – a big three-bedroom apartment right on the old campus.

You feel immediately welcomed in Ireland, especially if you are American. There are 3.5 million Irish and 30 million Irish descendants in the U.S.A. When customs checked my passport on my second trip, the official said. "Welcome back, Garrett!" When you leave Dublin Airport, you go immediately through American customs, avoiding it in the U.S. I asked the clerk if that meant Ireland was part of America or if America was part of Ireland. He replied, "Well, now; if I knew that I'd know everything!"

I loved talking to the Irish cab drivers on the trip to and from the airport. I asked the first how things were in his country. "We're BROOOOKE! We've got no money! And *now* the government is gonna tax the very air we breathe!" Passing a large bank, he pointed and said, "That's where the pirates live; they rob you with their fountain pens!"

I asked him about his religion, and he was a staunch Catholic, as was his father, going to Mass daily. "If someone had insulted a priest in front of me father, Old Dad would've killed him!"

One cab driver entertained me with so many funny stories on the way to the airport, that I gave him the 40 Euro fare and a 40 Euro tip. He stared at the money, looked at me, and said, "You're a *Gentleman*, Sar!"

In my lodgings at Trinity, I was looked after by an old, fat Irish housekeeper, "Ria" (from "Maria"). She talked continually about every personal subject; cleaned the digs at all times of day; sat down to have a "cup of tea" with me; and generally treated me like one of the family. Another staunch Irish Catholic, she joked when I expressed concern about the College placing a young woman visitor in my apartment. "Oh, don't worry; you might get lucky!"

She had an ongoing war with her supervisor, who accused her of stealing cleaning supplies. When I left, I asked how the dispute was going. She said, "Oh, fine. I've turned it into a little cat-and-mouse game. I'll hide a couple of rolls of toilet paper in the back of my cart and when she says they are missing, I pull them out and say, "These?!"

She also told me that the noises I heard nightly behind a bookshelf were not mice, but College ghosts. "But don't worry;

they're harmless in this House. Now that building next door has terrible ones. I won't go in there!"

Ria helped me to find things in Dublin and to pronounce such names as "Geaghahanen" (it's pronounced "Ge-gan"). I asked her why I couldn't find an Irish fairy statuette for my daughter while Leprechauns abounded in the shops. She said, "Well, fairies are what we call 'The Little People' and they're invisible." I'm reminded of the invisible rabbit "Pooka" in the Jimmy Stewart movie *Harvey*.

We became very close friends – almost family, as the Irish "adopt" almost everyone.

The lodging's kitchen was furnished with dishes and utensils, but I'd bought a few large things: a teapot, pans, and knives. They were too large to bring home, so I told Ria I'd just leave them for the next resident. She looked very sad at my leaving. Asking plaintively, "Won't you be coming back next year?"

I replied (though it was unlikely), "Oh, yes, probably."

She smiled and said, "Well, I'll pack them up in a box with your name on it, and they'll be here for you when you return."

I encountered so many instances of such warmth, kindness, and friendship in Ireland. Once, while walking to the College theater one evening (to see Noel Coward's play *Present Laughter*) I was approached by an Irishman who asked me, "Do you know the way to the theater?"

"Yes, I'm going there, come along with me. Are you seeing the play?"

"Oh, yes," he said, "I *have* to; me wife's in it," I explained that I had many performers in my family and attended many plays. "Yo," he said, "and that makes us the best actors, 'cause we always tell 'em they did a good job!"

My family came to stay with me for a couple of weeks, during my three-month sabbatical in Ireland and I recall a train trip to Galway, watching the countryside and visiting the historic town where many Irish left for America. Several Catholic churches there had hours of Confession rather than Mass! My son, a musician, especially enjoyed the lively music in restaurants and pubs.

I visited both Anglican Cathedrals in Dublin: Christ Church and St. Patrick; (it seems the British could return ONE to Catholic Ireland) but worshipped regularly at Christ Church. It reminded me of my Anglo-Catholic upbringing: glorious architecture, choir, organ, stained glass, Holy Communion. The Head Priest had the most delightful Anglo-Irish accent: smooth, soft. My last Sunday, I expressed my appreciation to him, and he replied, "Well, it was a pleasure to have your attendance."

In spite of one Sunday, when I tried to enter the church, a doorman (a monk, I think) practically barred me from the door. "They're havin' service in there, you know." (Thinking I was an American tourist?) "I know," I said. He shouted, "It'll be at least an hour and a half long!" I assured him I'd been there before and knew this. Finally, he reluctantly gave me a program and let me enter.

My sabbatical research was to be on Edmund Burke, the Conservative political theorist whose papers were in the Trinity College Archives. I didn't have a topic in mind, just to see what I'd find in his papers worthy of study and possibly publication. You had to get special permission and wear white gloves to examine these historic documents. Most were familiar, but one was unknown to me: The College Debate Club book of which Burke was secretary as a student. Just reading his original, hand-written notes was awesome to me.

I discovered nothing new, however, until I met with the Dean, Patrick G., a Burke scholar. He was a brilliant and delightful person and asked my areas of interest. I said Political Theory, Law, and Religion. "Well," he said, "there hasn't been much written on Burke's religion or its relation to his political thought." That spurred me on to research and ended in an article on "Burke's Catholic Conservatism" in the journal *Modern Age* a year later. (Summer, 2014) This study drew upon many of Burke's lesser-known writings and a recent biography *Edmund Burke; The First Conservative*, by Jessee Norman. My background in Political Theology helped, as the Augustinian influence was very important.

The trick was to show how Burke, who had to be Protestant to serve in the British Parliament, could be Catholic in breeding, education, and sentiments. This was also confirmed by a "chance" conversation at a coffee house in the catacombs of the Cathedral after Sunday Service when I spoke with a Visiting Scholar from Australia who mentioned other books making this argument.

I recall, after much study, having the whole outline of the article come to me as I was walking from the College swimming pool to my rooms; sitting down on a bench; and writing it on a scrap of paper in my pocket! Since then, the piece has been cited in several studies on Burke and religion.

Another "chance" encounter confirmed this thesis. I was in a small food shop one Sunday after church and the proprietor (as often happens in Ireland) struck up a conversation, asking who I was; what I was doing in Dublin; etc. When I described my research, he said he'd heard of Burke but knew little about him. He asked, "Was he Irish or ENGLIIIIIIIIIIIIIIIIISH?" (spitting out the last word with disdain).

I said, "Well, he was raised in Ireland, but spent most of his adult life in England, in Parliament."

"Was he Catholic or PROTESSSSSSSSSSSSSTANT?!!!"

"Well," I said "that's an interesting question, and the main subject of my research. He was raised Anglican (Catholicism being illegal in 18th Century Ireland) and served in the British Parliament (where you had to affirm the Protestant faith), but his mother was Catholic, and his wife was Catholic. What do you think?"

The shopkeeper winked at me and whispered, "He was CATHOLIC!"

My leaving of the Irish told of their character. I had an early flight and had to leave Trinity College before the Housing Office opened that morning. I told the clerk and asked, "Where should I leave my room key? With Campus Security? With your office slipped under the door? In my room?" The official smiled and said, "Oh, whatever you like!" This casual, sensible attitude, contrasting American or British Rules and Regulations is why I love Ireland and the Irish so much.

My published research from this Irish sabbatical led to my next trip – to Australia and The Burke Society.

Melbourne, Australia

Somehow that Burke article in the journal *Modern Age* found its way to Australia and someone passed it on to the President of the Edmund Burke Club, Gerard Wilson. He emailed me and a long, lively correspondence led to an invitation to address the club in February 2015. It was one of the greatest experiences of my life. I left a snow and ice blizzard in mid-winter and arrived "Down Under" in a hot mid-summer in Australia.

As the plane descended on Melbourne, I saw the most wild, exotic landscape I'd ever seen. Jungles, high peaks, lakes, desert, and a great modern city on the ocean coast.

My host, a publisher with an M.A. in Philosophy, greeted me warmly at the airport and I was whisked (after a 35-hour flight) to a lovely hotel near a residential area, where I often walked to the sight of palm trees and sounds of exotic jungle birds. Never saw a kangaroo, though. The "Aussies" were a friendly, kind people, like the Irish from which many descended. It was originally a British Penal Colony (which in the 18th Century meant the outlawed Catholics and many minor London criminals).

Gerard's Catholic family, like my New England Puritan ancestors, was amongst the first settlers in Australia. His many-volume autobiography detailed the fascinating history of his family. Besides being a devout Catholic, Gerard was active in Conservative politics and a Burke scholar. We became fast friends and have continued in contact ever since.

He arranged a dinner at the Savage Club – modeled on a traditional English Men's Club in London – where the Burkeans met. Dinner was in a small, elegant wood-paneled dining room (after drinks in the "parlor") after which I gave my paper on "Constituting the Constitution": the traditional British Cultural Constitution that Burke's Conservative thought expressed. (*Harvard Journal of Law 20*). Afterward, I received many intelligent questions and comments from members, and the most beautiful tribute by a Roman Catholic priest who rejoiced in our "fellow brother of the British Commonwealth" and my illumination of our common heritage. More papers and reports followed, then, the evening ended with glasses of port back in the parlor and conversation. Very civilized and pleasant.

The next day, we had a Conference on Burke at La Trobe University, at which I gave the Keynote Address from my "Burke's Catholic Conservatism" article. Another great discussion, other papers, and a great lunch.

Of all the countries I've visited, I think Australia most resembles the U.S.A. Friendly, casual, and democratic.

And it is one of the few I would like to visit again. (If it weren't for that 35-hour flight!) But I feel blessed and grateful to have made that trip and to have those experiences.

CHURCH

The "True Church" is all people who believe, by Faith, the essentials of Christianity, regardless of denomination. This is what C. S. Lewis described in his book *Mere Christianity* – those central beliefs or doctrines common to all churches, which may differ in the finer points of theology or governance. Lewis sent his book to the main denominations in England: Catholic, Anglican, Methodist, and Presbyterian and all accepted his summary of the essentials of the Faith.

Those essentials of Christianity are that every human is sinful: disobedient to God's Law and Spirit; secretly believing and wanting to BE God; all-powerful, all-controlling, and worshipped by others. This "Original Sin" of Pride and Self-Idolatry leads to "The Fall" as described in the first book of the Bible, Genesis, which leads to Adam and Eve's loss of Paradise and every other sin (murder, lying, stealing, adultery, etc., etc.). All the cruelty and misery in the world is rightly punished, ultimately by separation from a Holy God, Death, and Hell.

But God so loved His beings made "in His own image" (reason, creativity) that He Himself came to earth as a human (Jesus) – the only man WITHOUT sin, so He could take our sin, and its punishment, upon Himself, on the Cross. And by Faith in that love and sacrifice, we can have forgiveness of our sins; can enter an Eternal Heaven with a Holy God after our death here; and even have a bit of Heaven here in this life by the "indwelling" of God's Holy Spirit in Believers.

The Church is that Body of Believers, led by Christ's Spirit, not perfect on this earth, with still-flawed humans, but a Community of Faith to teach, support, and love its members and the world at large. So, the classic "conversion experience" is when someone (like St. Paul) is "convicted" of his or her sin, repents of it, receives God's grace and forgiveness, and begins a New Life. Growth in that Faith is a lifetime, probably eternal, process and the Church is to offer knowledge, guidance, and encouragement (of confession, repentance, love, charity, forgiveness, etc.) through its teachings, and example in classes, sermons, music, worship, counseling, and prayer.

My Church experience has been wide and varied: from Anglo-Catholic Episcopal to Protestant Baptist Evangelical, with Mainline Presbyterian, Pentecostal, Non-denominational Charismatic, and Methodist mixed in! This is why I am "Ecumenical"; at home in any Christian denomination and having received blessings and advancements from each.

I grew up in the Episcopal Church (St. Paul's) in Milwaukee, Wisconsin, in the 1950s and 60's. (Baptized by the Bishop of the Diocese a few days after my birth.) For some reason, this American branch of the Anglican Church of England in the Upper-Mid-West United States at that time was all High Church or Anglo-Catholic. Emphasis on Ritual, Creeds, Liturgy, Hierarchy, a celibate clergy (priests), the Mass (Holy Communion), incense, sacred music, mystery, order, dignity, and beauty. It was like growing up English Catholic – including being in the Boys Choir. As I describe it in my Chapter "Ritual and Liturgy" in the book *Retreat of the Soul*, it gave me a sense of the majesty of God, His mystery, power, awesomeness (and goodness, love, and protection). The *1928 Book of Common Prayer* expresses this. An otherworldly, elegant, aristocratic, artistic church captured in the YouTube video "Virtual Tour of St. Paul's Milwaukee Church, Milwaukee." That decorum affected my whole life, even though I never heard the gospel "preached" – it was conveyed in Creeds and Prayers and Sacraments.

It may be that this "High" Episcopal Church in that area and time was due to "The Oxford Movement" in the mid-1800s in England that strove to regain the Catholic heritage. It has largely disappeared in the Liberal Episcopal U.S.A. Church, except for break-away "Anglican" congregations.

When my family moved to the suburbs of Mequon, Wisconsin we attended a much smaller, newer, more humble Episcopal Church than the grand stone English Gothic Cathedral of St. Paul's. But I remember the priest, Father A., and his devotion, including to my troubled family, through visits and counseling.

When we moved to Albuquerque, we again attended a newer, small Episcopal Church, still Liturgical but much more unimpressive.

When I went to college, as do many young people "on their own" I stopped attending church, though I didn't lose my Faith despite the usual young radical's skepticism.

It was in 1980, seven years later, that I returned to church. Married and living in Princeton, N. J. (where Elaine, my wife, was enrolled at Princeton Theological Seminary) I attended "the Seminary Church" Nassau Presbyterian, an old colonial church next to Princeton University, historic in its Neo-Classical, Greek Revival architecture (white columns, tall windows, white pews). There, I heard for the first time in person, evangelized preaching under the power of the Holy Spirit.

The minister, highly intellectual like the area, with a degree from Harvard Divinity School, nonetheless was from the South (Georgia) and his sermons were intense and emotional. I felt the power of God as I hadn't since hearing Billy Graham and, later, Charles Stanley on TV. The Rev. W. A.'s sermons frequently brought one to tears and greatly affected my spiritual growth.

When we moved to Virginia for my job at the College, we tried the local Presbyterian, Methodist, and Episcopal churches, settling in the last, All Saints' Episcopal in Norton, Virginia, where we stayed for about ten years. It was a small, close congregation, full of "characters", fun, and laughter, along with devotion to the old faith, music, and liturgy. I also became involved in church governance, serving on the Vestry as Senior Warden and on the Executive Board of the Diocese.

But by the 1980s, the American Episcopal Church was becoming very liberal, politically and theologically. Now with young children, we wanted them brought up in the Christian faith, and finally left for a large, non-denominational "charismatic" or Pentecostal church, part of an evangelical "Move of the Spirit" in America in the 1990's. This lively, loving church's openness to the Spirit of God (in healing, insight, gifts, and tongues) taught me much about the Third Person of the Trinity, especially being OPEN to God's leading in prayer and preaching.

During that time, I felt led to update my great-grandfather's (Charles M. Sheldon) famous Christian novel *In His Steps*, as *What Would Jesus Do?* (the theme of the story). This led to my being invited to speak at many evangelical churches (Southern Baptists seemed especially familiar with *In His Steps*, though it was published almost 100 years earlier). An article in the religious site *Patheos*, "*WWJD*? Sheldon's Great Grandson Still at It", describes this and how it led to my church ministry.

A small, country Baptist Church north of the College, Nash's Chapel, invited me to preach on *WWJD*. This was a tiny church made up primarily of retired coal miners and farmers descended from about five families in this rural area 100 years earlier. A very humble congregation. They kept inviting me back to preach, being without a pastor (and unable to afford one). Eventually, they asked ME to become their pastor. I said, "That is very kind, but I am not a Southern Baptist." Oh, they said, that doesn't matter; you preach the Gospel and care about us, and that's all we need in a pastor. So, I was ordained after an examination by local clergy and an ordination service with the "laying on of hands", prayers, a sermon by a prominent Baptist minister, and a reception.

I served for six years as a "bi-vocational" minister at that small, simple church. I thought God must have a sense of humor to take an Anglo-Catholic choir boy and make him a Southern Baptist "Preacher". Or perhaps His revenge, as I'd made fun of evangelicals most of my life. And, now, I was one.

This was also part of an Evangelical/Charismatic Revival in America in the 1990s, with the rise of televangelists; The Million Man March on Washington, D. C.; the charismatic movement even in mainline denominations (e. g. Presbyterian); and President George W. Bush expressing an evangelical faith.

At my first church, I learned the rudiments (and challenges) of ministry: services (funerals, weddings, baptisms, preaching, prayer, pastoral visits, etc.) as well as church conflicts (business meeting fights, jealousies, criticism, and church politics).

My upbringing in a Catholic Anglican liturgical tradition, as well as the reliance upon God's Holy Spirit from my Pentecostal experience, served me well in this ministry.

But, after six years, for a variety of reasons, I felt "released" from that ministry and I really thought, sadly, that I'd never be a pastor again.

We attended various evangelical/charismatic churches in our area (notably Zion Church of God and East Stone Gap Methodist, where we knew many people).

Then, after about a two-year hiatus, we joined First Baptist Church of Big Stone Gap (in the heart of our local town): a large, Neo-gothic structure with dark wood pews and altar, burgundy carpets, arched stained glass windows, and a glorious music program. It seemed God was indulging my aesthetic tastes. The membership, too, though down from the 500 of its hay day, was large and prosperous, educated and diverse. A devout yet friendly, intelligent group.

*This photograph of First Baptist Church
was taken by Elizabeth Steele
on Easter Monday, April 13, 2020*

About a year after I joined, the pastor left for another church and I was called upon (as the only ordained member) to guest-preach, visit the sick in the hospital, and conduct special services.

Then I was asked to be "interim pastor" as they searched for a full-time minister. Then I was asked to be that minister. I said that I couldn't as I had a full-time job at the college and could not fairly serve such a large church as its only pastor.

Someone suggested hiring an associate pastor, to do much of the work as I became the senior pastor – his getting most of the salary, the minister's house (parsonage across from the church), and filling in for me as I was frequently away on academic trips. We "called" a young pastor who had studied at Liberty University.

This worked with mixed results for about three years and then he left to be a youth minister at a large church in Eastern Virginia.

The church tried to replace him, but after a long search found no one suitable. So, we adopted a "Team Ministry" with various leaders in music, administration, youth ministry, and finance. Fortunately, this church had an unusually large number of very capable and devoted members who looked after the hospitality, maintenance, missions, business, decoration, etc. of the parish. Several members could serve not only the Deaconate of helping needy parishioners but also pray and preach when I was away. It was my ideal of "The Church" – The Body of Christ with participants of diverse gifts from God, serving faithfully and co-operatively to spread the Gospel, extending charity to the needy inside and outside the church, and being a "spiritual family".

Though not perfect, this has been the most truly Christian church I've ever known. Visitors often say they feel the Spirit of Christ when they enter – of love, joy and peace. I don't know why God has blessed us so, but it is the closest to the ideal Christian church I've ever known – balancing tradition, the Bible, and an openness to the Holy Spirit.

I've been the minister at First Baptist Church, Big Stone Gap, for about 14 years now. We've weathered many changes, including the COVID-19 Virus (when we kept Sunday services going continually) and changing demographics. I don't know what the future will bring, but I trust in God's care and providence. I expect I will remain until I "see out" that generation who brought me in – probably four or so more years, at the Biblical lifespan of three-score and ten (70 years old).

SPIRITUAL EXPERIENCES

I have witnessed many miracles: of healing, changes, reconciliation, and visions. I cannot explain them, especially why some prayers led to healing (of cancer, organ correction, recovery) and others seem not to, except that "all things work together for good..." (Romans 8:28) And that, in the old Anglican prayer, "God hears every prayer of His children, and answers every prayer in the time and way best for us."

The Beatific Vision

Perhaps the most memorable miracle was when I had a vision of God. It was when we were worshipping in that large inter-denominational charismatic church which was designed like a large tent with bullet lights on the ceiling shining down. We always gathered together at the front of the large sanctuary to pray before the altars. I was standing, eyes closed, lifted towards the ceiling, hands at my side, palms facing upwards. Suddenly, I had a vision of Christ on His throne in Heaven, all radiating beams of golden light yet in clearly defined lines. I cannot describe it because it was an image you could not represent or create in this world: both all flowing light and clear definitive lines. Such an image is only possible in Heaven. I have seen pictures since of the Sacred Heart of Jesus with beams of light streaming out of His heart, but never the simultaneous all-light but clear definition.

I since have read of this "Beatific Vision" (Vision of God) that others have had but know now why I was blessed by it at that time. I told no one about it. I even went the next Sunday to the same spot and assumed the same posture, thinking it might just be the ceiling lights on my eyes. It wasn't. I've told only a few. But afterward my "faith" was "by sight" as well as belief.

We don't know why certain Saints were given this vision. It might just be a gift from God. It might be to prepare us for some task or ministry. It occurred right before I was to travel to Moscow, Russia. Perhaps it was to prepare me for this (an exciting but scary trip – during which I wore a small wooden cross under my shirt).

It is the greatest spiritual experience I have had.

Death

Another one occurred in my late 30's.

I'd had severe chest pains that morning; my wife drove me to the hospital emergency room. I was hooked up to a heart monitor.

Suddenly I felt very faint and told the nurse.

Elaine in the waiting room heard the frantic announcement, "CODE BLUE!"

My heart stopped.

Then I died.

I felt a profound peace as I drifted out of this life. Then I saw myself sitting with another man, his foot up on a wall, talking to me. I don't know if it was an angel, Jesus, or someone in heaven.

Suddenly I was jolted back to life, my heart restarted, and I felt all the cares, stress, and pain of this world come upon me. I was awake. The attending nurse was looking down on me with tears in her eyes. I was kept in hospital for about a week and had many tests, but no major problems were found.

But I will never fear dying now. It was peace, joy, rest.

Bardstown Brothers

One of the greatest Christian experiences of my life has been a group of ministers who go on a Retreat every year to a Catholic monastery: The Abbey at Gethsemane in Bardstown, Kentucky. Revs. Jim Wells, Greg Sergent; Jeff Noel, and others (about ten) from many different denominations for a few days in October at the Guest Home of the nearby Sisters of Charity Convent, just talking, praying, attending Compline; walking the beautiful grounds, visiting churches and "Mammy's" – a wonderful restaurant. It is a time of spiritual refreshment for us "Bardstown Brothers" and affects the rest of the year. We're close friends, sharing needs, problems, and laughter.

One ritual was to stop at a nearby grocery store to get "snacks" for our time there. One evening a few of us had finished our shopping and were standing at the store entrance waiting for the others. A woman walked in and stared at us – four old men holding our grocery bags. She said, "Who are YOU all?"

Jeff replied, "Someone at The Home left the door unlocked."

About five years ago one of our group, Greg Sergent, a dear longtime friend, suggested we compile a book on *The Contemplative Life* from our experiences at the Retreat and our ministries. Each of us wrote a chapter on our "specialty" (mine on Liturgy and Ritual) that was published as *Retreat of the Soul*. It has not exactly been a bestseller, but it has sold all over the world and I believe God has used it to encourage the contemplative prayer and spirituality we saw in the monks at the Abbey.

I am grateful for the Faith God has given me and the variety of religious experiences in the many churches in which He has placed me.

As I've written this chapter, as with this entire *Memoir*, I can see God's Providence, Purpose, and Plan for my life, His Humble Servant.

FRIENDS

Throughout my life, I have been blessed with friends. Not a great number; not "the gang" or the "in crowd" of the school or organization. But a few (2-5) VERY close friends, with whom one could play, trade, have fun with, especially talk and laugh. Very close means "confidants" – with whom you could share anything: your hopes, fears, anger, joy, news.

In Grammar School it was a few pals who lived in the neighborhood: walking to school together; building snow forts; having snowball fights; sledding; swimming; trading comic books; and staying over at each other's houses for meals and sleepovers.

In Middle and High School: sports, clubs, trips, parties, sharing stories of girls, beer, dreams, and smoking.

In College and Graduate School; discussing ideas, politics, philosophy, religion, ambitions, jokes, imitations.

Early in my career, as I mentioned, the Junior Faculty Caucus, met to talk, gossip, drink, laugh, and support one another. In my later life, academic and church colleagues who talk on the phone, message, have lunch, tea, talk, commiserate, and share. Rev. Greg Sergent and Professor Jeff Morrison come to mind. As St. Paul described ideal Christians: share each other's joys and bear each other's burdens.

As the ancient Greek Philosopher Aristotle described in his *Ethics*: "philia" – a particularly close, deep friendship, where we share a common view and perspective, we see things similarly and so can UNDERSTAND each other and BE understood by others. Very important for personality development, comfort, guidance, and therapy, especially in times of trouble or trial.

C. S. Lewis describes this *philia* friendship in his book *The Four Loves* as looking in the same direction: seeing things the same way and so able to communicate. Unlike *eros* or romantic love, when the two stare at *each other*, especially during the infatuation stage, young love, "under the spell" or "ether" (which lasts between 6 and 18 months), deep friendship lasts a lifetime. *Agape* or God's (unconditional) love is similar but more perfect; *storge* love is just familiarity or long acquaintanceship, which *philia* will have eventually. One jokes that friends long separated just "start up where they left off" even if they haven't seen each other for years. As though no time has passed.

One such friend, who, sadly, just died suddenly, was Jim Whelpton ("Jimbo") whose family had a cottage next to ours in Michigan, so we grew up together every summer.

The Bardstown Brothers mentioned in the "Church" chapter is such a group of friends.

The C.C.C.C. (Congregational Civilized Conversation Club) or "Old Men's Club" as I call it: mostly retired men meeting once a week in the Archives House of the Congregational Summer Assembly to have "discussions", hear presentations, joke, and laugh. Camaraderie. Two C.C.C.C. sessions I recall fondly were when our jolly leader Jim Royale asked the ten members if they had continued the plans they started in college. All but one hadn't and the stories were hilarious. And when I was about to retire and asked them what I should expect. Very funny but valuable advice.

Most of these friendships were all male (boys will be boys) but occasionally they were "mixed-gender" as the grad school group "The Schlocks" mentioned in the "Education" chapter.

In all cases, these friendships added richness and comfort to life. It is no wonder that Jesus Christ, our Lord and Savior and God, told his disciples: "I call you friends."

JOBS

As Nelson Aldrich says in his book *Old Money*, families of my background: established, educated, "bourgeois" set for their children (especially boys) "ordeals" or "trials" to toughen up these privileged youth. Sports, lessons, and especially working-class jobs (after school and during summer) were to show us the harder side of life and society, to make us appreciate how many average people lived, struggled, and suffered, to make us appreciate our comforts and advantages. We learned to sympathize with "how the other half lives" (and have been a Big Tipper ever since) and to motivate us to do well in school, so we could climb out of that hard-working life into a more easy, comfortable, and prosperous professional careers (law, medicine, teaching, ministry, business, etc.).

Even as a small boy, I had "chores" – had to "earn" my small allowance through hard work (emptying trash cans, cleaning my room, mowing the lawn, etc.). That's how a Protestant Work Ethic and "the value of money" were instilled in us.

Beginning in high school, I had various after-school jobs involving considerable labor and low wages. My first was as a busboy at a large popular restaurant in a mall in Albuquerque, New Mexico. My shift was always afternoon and evening. I found my first night this was highly fluid, dependent on the crowd in the restaurant. I was supposed to get off at 11:00 p.m. and worked until 2:00 a.m. on a Friday night. Exhausting.

The bus boy cleared the tables of dirty dishes after diners left (under the careful eye of waitresses ensuring you didn't pocket their tips). Then haul the dirty dishes to the kitchen, loading them into a large conveyor belt dishwasher, and drying and stacking them for use by new diners. The bus boy was on the "bottom of the totem pole" – below managers, cooks, waitresses, and customers – all yelling at you.

My first night, after rushing about at these tasks for about four hours, about to collapse from exhaustion, I asked the manager when we got a "break". He just laughed. No one was nice or kind to me save for a young cook, who inquired as to my name.

That job lasted about two months. To this day, I am extremely courteous and generous to restaurant personnel.

My next high school job was at the arrangement of one of my father's acquaintances (as his father had done for him and his father for him – I could go father – I mean farther); manual labor in a reed factory. This was a small factory ("sweatshop") adjoining a man's house making reeds for musical instruments (oboes, trombones, clarinets, etc.). I sat on a stool and worked on "The Gouger" on a table before me. This entailed taking a short bamboo rod (split in two) from a box to the left of me, placing it in a metal groove on the machine tipping a handle with a blade attached to a crank, and "gouging" out the soft center of the bamboo to a certain size and then dropping it in a box to the right of me. Cranking, cranking, cranking, for hours. (Sometimes I awake at night, my arm "cranking" the gouger.) This job lasted a couple of years until I entered college.

Then I got a job as a "pump jockey" at a gas station. Back then you pulled into a gas station, and someone (like Gomer Pyle) came out, filled up your tank, washed your windshield, and checked your oil. No convenience store. A mechanical shop adjoined where you worked when not pumping gas.

Mostly in college, I got financial aid and only worked summers. One summer, I worked as a Line Man at a small private airport north of Albuquerque, where my father kept his plane. This job also involved pumping gas (but into airplanes) atop a fuel truck. Also, towing planes and answering the radio to give descending planes the wind direction and landing instructions. I recall the eight-hour shifts were variable, depending on demand. I liked the graveyard shift (11:00 p.m. – 7:00 a.m.) because it was quiet and empty, so I could catch up on my reading. But constant changing of work shifts caused problems with sleep cycles.

In college, I also worked as a Real Estate salesman (also thanks to one of my father's friends) and learned I didn't like the vagaries of commission sales income or salesmanship. This job did have the advantage of showing me what most lawyers did: boring contracts, and business. Just as I was getting interested in academics, this provided more incentive to avoid law school.

In grad school, I got some jobs associated with the university (research, grants, programs at Rutgers) but also some private jobs. One summer I worked for a marketing firm testing products (food, liquor) on potential customers (in malls, shops) or telephone polling for public issue surveys. I recall the impatience and angry profanity yelled at us "Telemarketers". Again, I have been polite to them ever since. Occasionally this work involved delivering mailers to homes, giving me an acquaintance with vicious dogs.

Although I hated most of these jobs ("ordeals" at the time) they were expected of most Middle-Class American youth and "built character". I didn't push such employment on my children, and they seem to have found them on their own and have fine work ethics, without their father's encouragement.

"CHARACTERS I HAVE KNOWN"

NaNa

The most important person in my life was my "Nana" or paternal grandmother, Cornelia Kellogg Sheldon. She was the most generous, intelligent, charming, gracious, funny, special person I have ever known. The stability and security (emotional, social, material, moral) kept us younger ones in the family safe and happy despite our parents' problems, weaknesses, and dysfunctional marriage.

NaNa's home was a haven of
peace, beauty, calm, plenty, and joy.

She had studied art at Wellesley College in the early 20th Century and her taste in design was elegant but understated, comfortable, and beautiful, like her manners. Growing up in a prominent family in the Victorian Era, she had very high standards, but her formality was tempered by warmth and humor. The perfect blend of tradition and spontaneity.

One truly remarkable thing about her was that she treated us kids not as the ignorant, willful children that we were, but as rational adults. (Which we definitely were not!) Her intelligent, frank conversation caused us to try to be like her, and act more grown-up than we were, more mature and civilized.

She had a natural affinity for young people. It was a joke that when she took her two young children to the nearby Clody Park, all the neighborhood children followed along, like the pied piper.

She took us to get new school clothes in September, gave us spending money for travel and vacations, and bailed me out with large sums when my house building went way over budget, or I was broke between college semesters.

Mostly, she was the most pleasant person to be around. When we'd mention we loved visiting her when we'd grown up, she would reply graciously, "I'm glad I have a home that my grandchildren like to visit."

She had an inbred stoicism, never betraying any feelings of fear, grief, or anger in public, despite some very great personal tragedies in her life. Her conversation was uplifting, charming, and witty. A delightful voice and laugh.

Once, when I was a teen, I asked her about love and romance. She told me how her husband, my grandpa, was an extraordinarily handsome young man, which people frequently commented on. She would reply, "Well, not just anybody could have caught him!"

She was in college and an early bride in the "Roaring Twenties" and a bit of a "Flapper". I recall her often singing the 1920s Cole Porter song "Anything Goes" while doing dishes.

She was an exceptionally strong, competent woman: a leader in the community and church, but a conservative traditional wife and mother who eschewed modern Feminism. A bit like the Empress Dowager in *Downton Abbey*.

We loved having afternoon tea (and later gin and tonic) in her beautiful, comfortable living room or, in the summer, on the screened porch off the back of the house. Conversation was a social activity before TV, cell phones, and computers. We learned so much from her in those talks. Once, when I confessed to her that I found my hereditary premature gray hair (at age 16!)

bothered me, she replied, "Oh, don't worry, dear. gray hair looks nice on a young face. It doesn't look so good on an old face."

Once, when she was reading a children's story to me as a little boy, I noticed the "age spots" on the backs of her hands and asked what they were. She said, "Oh, those are the spots that say I'm an old lady." She was probably in her early 60s at the time but always looked younger. Tall and erect with strong features, she was still attractive at her death at 100 years old. I visited her shortly before she died in hospital as she had fallen and broken a hip. She had Alzheimer's but still recognized me and eagerly responded when I offered to pray for her.

She died peacefully about thirty years ago and a day doesn't go by when I don't think of her and thank God for her. A Memorial Service was held for her at Christ Episcopal Church in Whitefish Bay, Wisconsin, but I couldn't bring myself to go and say, "Goodbye."

Fortunately, as in most families, her memory lives on in other family members who resemble her, notably my sister Barbara and my daughter Gwendolyn. The latter, especially, is almost the identical image of Nana, in appearance, personality, and actions. So, I still am reminded often of my beloved Nana, who lives on in my heart.

Cary McWilliams

Wilson Cary McWilliams was my graduate advisor, mentor, and Ph.D. dissertation director at Rutgers. He is the closest thing to a genius I have ever known. With a photographic memory, he could recite long passages from the Bible, literature, and political speeches. We used to "trick" him by asking the most obscure details in American history (Who *was* the Secretary of State under President McKinley?) only to have him name him and discourse for thirty minutes on his background. To this specific knowledge, he added a deep understanding of Classical Political Theory and Theology. (The real meaning of that verse in the prophet Joel; or the Aristotelian term *thymos*; or John Adams' misunderstanding of Plato's *Republic*.) To this, he added a humor and wit unmatched in any academic I know.

Once, lecturing on the American education advocate John Dewey, Cary said, "Dewey once remarked that he thought he was a Marxist, but had never read Marx; that does not necessarily mean he was a member of the Livingston College Sociology Department."

While visiting his house for a grad student event (teacher and students used to socialize together) his wife remarked on my blue-blazered, button-down collar, preppy appearance. "Doesn't Garrett look nice?"

"Yes, Cary said. "But look at his eyes: shrewd and guileful." At age 25, I was the *least* shrewd and guileful person in the world.

Once, when the Political Science Department was choosing a new Graduate Chair, Cary refused to be considered. "I wouldn't run if the only other candidate was Adolph Hitler!" And aside, "Or even S_ _ _ _!" (a department colleague).

At my doctoral dissertation defense, I went to the chalkboard and said to the committee, "I will outline the thesis so you can follow my arguments."

Carey replied, "Sheldon, we don't 'follow' your arguments, we 'experience' them!"

Despite this brilliant, often biting wit, Cary was one of the most genuinely compassionate men I have ever known. He was a world-renowned scholar of Historical Political Theory, Religion, Law, Politics, and American Political Thought; but often spent hours helping, supporting, and advising young academics and students. After I left and took a job at an obscure college in Appalachia, he visited several times to speak and consult. He once even lent me money.

His father had been very prominent in Liberal Democrat Politics during the New Deal in the 1930s, editing *The Nation* magazine. If Cary had one intellectual weakness, it was his fierce, irrational hatred of Republicans. Once, while living in Princeton, I mentioned that they were putting on Dickens' play *A Christmas Carol*. Cary shouted, "All the Republicans will be cheering for Scrooge!" He would turn purple with rage when anyone mentioned Reagan favorably.

Despite his Liberal politics, he was a Cultural Conservative, a staunch traditional Presbyterian, and a lover of the Tory philosophy of Edmund Burke. He wrote and lectured profusely, including at Harvard, and sent an army of Political Theory students to universities all over America.

He always had a crowd of admirers around him, but I was blessed to spend a two-hour dinner alone with him at the Alchemist and Barrister Restaurant in Princeton shortly before his death. He died suddenly of a heart attack in his 60s while changing a flat tire on his car on the way to lecture at Hunter College. Flags were flown at half-mast at Rutgers. I could not bear to attend his Memorial at the Old Chapel there; but, as with my Nana, I often think of him and smile. Like the time I (with a group of students and professors) in a pub in New Brunswick offered to buy him a beer, Cary replied, "Beer?!! Beer is for Germans and graduate students!"

At the time (like all youth) I had no idea how extraordinary he and other professors at Rutgers were. I have noticed the difference in the quality of college professors lies in the quality of their teachers in graduate school. I was blessed with a "world-class" faculty at Rutgers and their worldwide exposure, research publications, scholarship, and experience greatly blessed me. How fortuitous (or providential) was my having a teacher and mentor in American Political Theory, Religion, Politics, and Law of the caliber of Cary McWilliams?

Professor E. L. (Edward Lee) "Buck" Henson

My principal guide and mentor when I was a young Ph.D. "know-it-all" Assistant Professor was an elderly Senior Professor of History at Clinch Valley College: E. L. "Buck" Henson. Buck was the quintessential old professor: tall, thin, tweed jacketed, squinting, absent-minded, dedicated. The College was his life. He was an Academic. At College events, he was the first to arrive and the last to leave. I recall my first Commencement at CVC on the big lawn by the lake. After all the graduates, parents, and faculty had left and the kitchen staff was cleaning up after the reception, "Old Buck" and I lingered, talking about the College, history, and life.

He grew up a Southern Gentleman in Lexington, Virginia; attended VMI (Virginia Military Institute); served in Europe as a Major in WWII; taught at a military academy near Charlottesville while he studied for a Ph.D. in History. His specialty was American Diplomatic History.

His antics in the classroom were legendary. Obscure quotations, questions, jokes, puns. A group of his male students said they attended "Uncle Buck's School for Wayward Boys". He dressed and spoke formally, addressing his students as "Mr." and "Miss" and their last names. To a student who used a lot of foul language in class, he said, "Mr. _ _ _, could we have a bit less of the barnyard language?"

Once, a radical sociology professor put a notice of his Colloquium lecture on "Marxian Hermeneutics and Sociology" on the History Department bulletin board. Buck took it down and hung up a notice: "Please do not post any notices with the word 'Hermeneutics' in it on the board."

The other "old boys" in the History Department who regularly gathered in his office to talk, painted on the back of a World War I army wheelchair, "The Buck Henson Chair of History".

While on a history field trip, Dr. Henson was driving a state car in a rainstorm. After the rain had stopped, he neglected to turn off the wipers until the student sitting in the front with him remarked, "Professor Henson, one thing you can say about these state cars: the windshield wipers sure work good!" After another five minutes, Buck turned them off and said, "Mr. _ _ _ _, are you trying to tell me something?"

At a faculty Colloquium when a biology professor was detailing his research on beavers in Michigan, Buck raised his hand and asked, "Phil, would you describe your subjects as 'busy'?"

Buck Henson was a special guy.

INTERVIEWS AND HEADHUNTERS

Although I spent my entire academic career at one place (Clinch Valley College of the University of Virginia or the University of Virginia's College at Wise) I interviewed at several other colleges and universities. Now I am glad I didn't move. But it seemed that the places I wanted to go to didn't want me and the places that wanted me I didn't want to go!

Especially in the 1990s (after I had written *What Would Jesus Do?*) I committed to gearing my teaching and scholarship to subjects somehow related to Christianity and the Church. This is not hard to do as the History of Political Theory, Political Theology; Religion and Politics, Constitutionalism, and even Law – are all related somehow to the Faith.

But I felt that, as a Christian academic, I should be at a Christian college. My last academic book, *The Political Philosophy of James Madison* (Johns Hopkins University Press) emphasized the theological foundations of Early American Political Thought and the U.S. Constitution, and it seemed I should be associated with a Christian college.

I interviewed at several Christian colleges, especially in the Midwest (where I also wanted to return "home"), and found they were not what I expected. To me, they would be filled with "C. S. Lewis's" – intellectually and spiritually very advanced; but I found them narrowly denominational (associated with one church or movement) and not the most outstanding academically. I am not politically or theologically Liberal, but my ecumenical and high scholarship approach was out of place at most of these institutions. I had one Dean at a very prominent Christian college in the Midwest tell me, "You wouldn't like it here." I thought of asking her if I could make that decision, but I think she meant I wouldn't "fit in". It seemed I could be more of a Christian academic, as I saw it, at a secular, public university!

But I wished to be in a Community of Faith in an academic setting, explicitly religious but very scholarly (as my evangelical Anglican College at Oxford, Wycliffe Hall, was when I was In Residence in 2002). A warm, loving society, but intellectually rigorous. The "best of both worlds", which doesn't seem to exist.

I've heard Notre Dame University is like that, but I've never been there.

My last attempt was a few years ago when I had my "headhunted" for a Christian university in Florida. A "Headhunter" is an executive or administrative recruiting company for businesses, foundations, and even universities. These recruiting agencies contact the top applicants, review their credentials, and do a rigorous series of phone and in-person interviews before recommending a top candidate to the hiring institution. I had been nominated for a top position at this university as both an Endowed Professor and Head of an Institute of Politics. I found the university and the positions VERY appealing, even though I was just a couple of years away from retirement at UVA-Wise.

The interviews, on the phone, in person in two places, and finally in Atlanta with the President and Provost were extensive and exhausting. When I described to my military officer brother he said, "That sounds like what I went through for a Top-Secret Security Clearance!" Every aspect of my life, career, family, research, etc. was scrutinized with questions, forms, reports, and references. It was an exciting experience I would never want to go through again.

Through it all, I still wanted very much to get the job. It was not offered to me. I have no idea why. But it was very disappointing after such a time- and energy-consuming endeavor. I was quite shocked and depressed.

But then, this rejection became a "blessing in disguise". I was most attracted to working with the provost, who was a brilliant, nice, funny, great guy. Then I learned the semester I would have started there he resigned to become President of a Christian college in the South. One of the main reasons I would have gone there disappeared. I finished my last few years at UVA-Wise and retired to our lovely home in the country, near a friendly small town, and where I am very happy now. As Romans 8:28 says, "All things work together for good for those who love God and are called according to His purposes."

LOVE, MARRIAGE, AND CHILDREN

Some things are too personal to write about. Suffice it to say, that I married the girl I fell in love with in college and we have remained together for over 40 years. We believe it was part of God's Providence and Grace and have had many blessings.

When I grew up, it was just expected that a person would get married and have children. Everyone did. Divorce was extremely rare; birth control was nonexistent. I didn't know there was any alternative. The American and Christian culture of my time was conservative, regarding marriage and family as the foundation of social order as well as personal fulfillment. And I'm glad it did. Although I was culturally caught between Chivalry and Feminism.

Henry James's 1884 novel *The Bostonians* describes this remarkably well. My English, aristocratic, Victorian Romanticism taught a "Gentleman's Code" towards women: to be polite, deferential, almost reverence towards women (who were the holders of virtue, charity, and morality) – never forcing one's attention on them, never taking advantage of them or manipulating them emotionally. This Medieval Chivalry view was partly based on the view of women as "the weaker sex" – to be protected and provided for.

By the 1970's New Feminism increasingly dominated America, with its views that men and women are equal in all ways; men should respect women as leaders in society, politics, business, the professions, etc., and traditional gender roles have oppressed and exploited women. The influence of both Chivalry and Feminism has made my relations with women complex.

Elaine has been a wonderful homemaker (as well as a teacher and advisor in dance, music, and arts) and especially a wonderful mother. She took care of all of the children's needs: food, clothes, education, health, finance, art performances, athletics, equipment, social activities (birthday parties, proms, celebrations), church, travels, pets, and anything else that might come up. I remember her sitting up all night with a sick child. Though now grown up, our children still call her if they have a need or problem. I attribute their being so talented, accomplished, and happy to their excellent mother.

No one is perfect, but the trials and tragedies of life were greatly mitigated by her motherly quality, which she inherited from HER mother, who was similarly loving and diligent.

I was present during the births of both of my children, Gwendolyn Mary and Peter John, and it is an experience that I will never forget. Children are a joy at every age, even with the hard work of parenting, challenges, and problems. Even as adults, with their own lives, they are a source of pleasure and meaning. For those called to have children (and not everyone is), it is like Aristotle's *telos*, or part of our destiny, fulfillment.

Marriage and family are part of God's plan for most (not all) people, as detailed in the Bible.

In the first book of the Bible, Genesis, God is shown to create Man (Adam) in His own image (with speech, reason, creativity). Then He saw that "it is not good for Man to be alone." So, God created the woman. In one version of this story, God puts Adam to sleep, opens his side, removes a rib, and makes a woman (Eve) out of it (why women used to be referred to as "Adam's Rib"). It is also the source of the old joke that the reason men don't understand women is because we were asleep when she was made!

God "created them, male and female". (Genesis 1:27) Their "gender roles" were that Eve was to be "a helper" to Adam. These roles were further defined after The Fall, when, as a consequence of their disobedience to God, they were expelled from Paradise, the Garden of Eden, and forced to work and struggle. The woman's curse is to bear children in pain, have a desire for her man, and be ruled by him. "Adam's Curse" is to work to "earn his bread by the sweat of his brow". (Genesis 3:16-19) These God-given role models: women giving primarily care to the children and home; and the husband working outside the home to support his family are the truth of natural law given at creation.

These natures will come out whether we deny them or not. Men have a natural aptitude to work and support their wives and children, to protect and defend. Women's "maternal instinct" is to care for others, provide, feed, etc. Even if they are not in a family context, I believe those traits will come out. Men rule, provide, and protect; women nurture and care for.

Jesus confirmed this (Matthew 19:4) when he said, "The Creator made them male and female. . ." Individuals vary in degrees of these characteristics. Some women have always worked outside the home (the Proverbial Good Wife is engaged in much commerce for her family – Proverbs 31:10-31) and some men are more "domestic" than others. I was blessed with a wife who took care of all the household matters (home, shopping, finances, etc.) freeing me to do my work of teaching, writing, speaking, preaching, traveling, and supporting the family. It was a good arrangement. A partnership.

The classic definition of the Christian marriage is in Ephesians 5:21-33 emphasizing that husbands "love" their wives and wives "respect" their husbands. Every couple who is married in my church is given a Bible and we mark and go over those Scriptures. That book of the Bible also details proper parent/child relations (Ephesians 6:1-4) that parents care for and raise, in morality, their children, and children obey and honor their parents. Most troubled marriages and families I have seen are due to not following these Godly principles. They are ideals that none of us imperfect humans can do, without the Grace of God, so the Christian principles of love and forgiveness are necessary.

REGIONS AND PLACES

I have lived in four distinct regions in the United States and one special place in the summer. Each had a unique social culture.

My first 13 years were spent in the Upper Midwest (Wisconsin); then 10 years in the Southwest (Albuquerque, New Mexico); six in the East (New Jersey, New York, New England); and almost 40 years in the South (Virginia).

The Northern Midwest where I grew up was a very traditional, conservative culture. Its settlers were Puritan New Englanders, Germans, and Poles. All orderly, religious, and serious. I recall the entire city of Milwaukee closing for Good Friday. Neat, clean houses, large, beautiful parks (on the Lake Michigan shore), an ornate, almost Baroque downtown, like a European city. Values of family, church, education, property, law, and respectability. In my chapter on Childhood, I described the emphasis on polite manners, deference, and quietude. Very safe, prosperous, and boring. Still, not a bad place to grow up, despite the cold winters.

The American Southwest, "Sunbelt", could not be much more different. Flat, dry, and brown, a new sprawling city built largely after WWII, settlers from all over the country overwhelmed the native Hispanic and Native American populations. Tacky, cheap buildings, large busy streets on a perfect north/west grid. Unimaginative, barren, and plain. No unifying culture, despite a preponderance of Hispanic (Mexican) and Southern "Anglo" (mostly Texan) populations. This did lend a variety, liveliness, and excitement absent in the predictable, stodgy Midwest. That, and the mild weather and constant sunshine, led to a light, cheerful mood.

The campus of the University of New Mexico was largely Spanish adobe style: clay buildings, flat roofs, and open squares, which had an aesthetic charm. As I mentioned in my chapter on "Education", this combination of warmth, casual atmospheres, and variety lent an open, creative atmosphere to learning, absent, especially, in old Eastern universities.

The Eastern United States, where I attended graduate school in New Jersey and New York, and spent much time with my sister's family in New England, is obviously "Old"— settled in the 1600s by Dutch English, Scots, and Germans; old buildings, old monuments, old customs, despite influxes of Irish, Italian, Black, Jewish, and other nationalities. I felt at home where my earliest ancestors settled when America was a colony, and reveled in the old colleges, towns, pubs, roads, villages, churches, and houses. The atmosphere was more antiquated and formal, despite constant changes in the past 400 years. Princeton was especially historic, with its Revolutionary past and pure Ivy League College.

The rural South (Virginia, the Appalachian Mountains near Kentucky and Tennessee) where I have spent most of my life (40 of the 67 years) is the most distinctive of any place I've lived. As I described coming here to take a job at a college in the chapter on "Career", I fell in love with the natural beauty of the mountains, the friendly and funny people, and the small-town flavor. When traveling, I'd often say, "I live in Mayberry", the typical Southern town of *The Andy Griffith Show*. Values of family, community, religion, music (Old Time/Bluegrass), humor (storytelling), friendliness, neighborliness (helping others), and loyalty still animate this region.

It is a comfortable life here, despite the problems of poverty, drugs (beginning with moonshine), and violence. It is a wonderful place to call home and my children are definitely "Wise Countians" despite their "foreign" parentage and wide travels.

Animals (dogs, horses, cattle, etc.), hunting, land, "country living", pick-up trucks, independence, equality, pride, and loyalty, mark this region. Acquaintances are not just functionaries (lawyers, doctors, ministers, postal carriers, teachers, mechanics, dentists, waitresses, accountants, merchants, barbers, police, politicians): they are friends. Like my physician, Dr. Tom Renfro, a fine Christian writer and minister. There is a *personal* quality to almost all relationships here that makes most areas (especially cities) seem cold and cruel. At best, in most areas people ignore you (albeit politely in the Midwest); at worst, they are hostile and dangerous. So, I feel blessed to have spent most of my life here.

No matter where I lived "in the winter", as we used to say, most summers I was at our family cottage in Northern Michigan. This "North Woods", like similar areas in Wisconsin and

Minnesota, is largely summer homes, lakes, and old forests. Our cottage, built by my Great-grandfather, Charles Sheldon, sits on top of a wooded hill, overlooking a small lake. It is part of a community known as "The Congregational Summer Assembly", founded by a group of ministers around 1900. This was common at this time in American history, of summer "Tent Revivals", ministers' retreats, and religious "Camp Meetings". It originally was made up of tents, then a lodge, and finally family cottages.

The Congregational clergy descended from the New England Puritan Church and still was designated as "Pilgrim", with roads like "Winthrop", "Edwards", and "Whitefield". Most of the cottages in the "C.S.A." are still owned by descendants of its founders; and although few are still clergy, the Reformed Christian flavor still exists, with ordinances against liquor, noise, radios on the beach, or unleashed dogs.

The original site of the church or Meeting House is still there at the center, with regular worship services, concerts, operettas, and even "Stunt Night".

It is a beautiful, peaceful, and even still spiritual atmosphere. Very restful, I often say that after just two days up there you feel like you've been on vacation for a month. Away from people, traffic, and noise, it is a true refuge from the world.

In the small family cottage are mementos (books, furniture, letters, journals, photos) from five generations of Sheldon's. You have to grow up there to appreciate it even in the rustic, often cold (in July!) atmosphere. Down "the hill" is a small beach on the clear, cold Crystal Lake. Clean, quiet, beautiful. There, as a boy, I learned to swim (shivering and looking blue), play tennis, and sail our small boat. Aldrich describes in his book *Old Money* this tradition of family cottages in the East (mostly in Maine) of "building character" and sailing as teaching one in navigation ("with" the wind, "against" it, without it, "becalmed"). A very free, but intensely organized, place.

One's "Right of Passage" was swimming across the Lake (3½ miles) usually in one's teens, after taking a Red Cross Life-Saving Class. That "swim" took about two hours, at the end of which one was so tired he could only crawl up on the opposite shore. My NaNa, with whom I regularly went to the cottage after my grandpa died, bribed me to take the challenge with a $5.00 reward and a cheeseburger at the A&W Root Beer Stand in a nearby town.

My kids participated in other organized sports (T-ball, soccer, tennis). They always had a Fourth of July celebration on the playing field with sack races, spoon races, and a "married men vs. single men" baseball game. Fireworks were set off all around the lake and at nearby Lake Michigan. Before that lake rose to cover its beach, we had family cookouts and watched the brilliant sunsets over the lake.

From my home in Virginia, it is a two- or three-day drive (now mostly on small country roads and small towns) but it is worth it. Getting away really gives one perspective on one's "normal" life. The cottage is usually shared by mice, bats, and (outside) raccoons, foxes, and deer. In the nearby town is wonderful fresh fish. My father's small sailboat (West Wight Potter) died with him, but I hope to soon replace it with a small cabin boat. A custodian family, who has taken care of the cottage since my grandfather's day, still keeps up the cottage.

There is something comfortable about such a familiar place. The friends you grew up with there still greet you every summer. A real *community* of shared past, values, and memories. A real blessing that I hope will stay in the family for many generations to come.

SPECIAL EVENTS

The White House

When I returned from the summer cottage in August of 2006, my college secretary, Linda M. handed me a note with a look as if to say, "You can believe this or not!"

It was a phone message from a Director of Special Initiatives at the White House asking me to call to arrange a meeting with President George W. Bush. I smiled as I thought of at least a dozen students and colleagues who could pull such a prank. Linda agreed but added, "But it did sound very official, so you should at least call him."

I did and sure enough, it seemed completely legitimate, and I arranged travel to Washington D. C. When I told my daughter Gwen she exclaimed, "THE WHITE HOUSE!" I want to go!"

It seemed that the President had some major world decisions to make, and he wanted to consult with a few scholars. Besides me was a British military historian (Oxford); a Classical historian (the now famous Conservative Commentator Victor Davis Hanson with whom I chatted in the Oval Office anteroom); and a Civil War Historian. I, apparently represented Early American Founding Ideology, as my book *The Political Philosophy of James Madison* had apparently made the rounds of the White House staff.

I entered extensive security at the East Gate with Marines looking at me like, "One false move, Buddy, and you're dead!"

President Bush struck me as both intelligent and kind, contrary to the Media's portrayal of him. The Oxford professor was in a wheelchair and the President asked how he was getting around, to which the Britain said his daughter accompanied him. Mr. Bush then said, "Well, let her come in", and she joined our group. We had a 90-minute "off the record" discussion about the state of the world and the U.S.A. It reminded me of a graduate school session with Bush the professor and we the students, as he asked questions, made observations, and offered insights. At the end (it was a Friday) he stood up and said, "Well, it's time for me to head to the Promised Land!" (Texas.)

I wandered around The White House for a while, found myself alone in a conference room, and had to ask a Black butler how to exit. My hotel was nearby, and I walked back as if in a dream. The dream of every professor: is to go to The White House to advise the President. He also generously had his photo taken with each of us and the copy of me shaking his hand adorned my College office to the astonishment of my students.

The next day I took a cab to the airport and returned home. In the cab as in two days before driven by an explicitly Arab Moslem I was intensely asked, "What are you doing in Washington?!!!"

"Oh, just some government business," I replied.

"WHAT KIND of government business?!!!" the driver inquired (as though he knew its importance) and I mumbled, "Oh, just some business . . ."

Back home I was able to divulge the purpose of my trip (but not the details) and was invited to address the Kiwanis Club in Wise.

A.I.P.A.C.

The American-Israel Public Affairs Committee is a lobby for U.S.–Israel relations. I became acquainted with them as a member of my church, Bobby T. was invited by them to visit Israel and he suggested I accompany them. At this time, as detailed in the chapter on Travels, Israel, AIPAC was sponsoring visits for American Evangelical Christians.

Yearly, AIPAC holds a Policy Conference in the big Convention Center in Washington, D.C. Eighteen thousand of God's original Chosen People (Jews), hundreds of events, meals, seminars, and meetings. Very intellectual, fascinating, and social. Like the Irish, Jewish people just come up to you and start talking, asking questions, etc.

At the end of two days of this activity, you are loaded into buses, and driven to the Capitol (Congress) to meet with your Representative and/or Senators. It is thrilling to walk the halls of Congress; and meet public officials, staff members, and fellow AIPAC enthusiasts.

At that time our relatively new Congressman, Morgan Griffith, a lawyer from Roanoke and Conservative Republican was the one I mostly talked with, and I found him intelligent, dedicated, and kind

My experience with the President (Executive), and Congress (Legislative) has been exciting and rewarding. But it confirms my Augustinian and Madisonian skepticism about worldly power – its seduction and corruption – and that my calling is academic, intellectual theoretical approaches to politics.

I admired those called to government service as the ideal of the American Republic (as I believe both President Bush and Congressman Griffith are), but it is an intense life that is too rich for me.

Outside the Capitol during the AIPAC Meeting.

HEALTH

I have turned into the "health nut" I always made fun of! Paying attention to diet, lifestyle, supplements, water (distilled), acupressure, etc. This didn't start until fairly recently. I enjoyed fine health most of my life except for a back injury in my 30s, lifting a heavy rug while moving house. Ever since, I have been in pain, if I have to stand or sit (especially in non-supportive chairs) for long periods of time. Lifting, bending, and even walking can set off a debilitating relapse.

But other than that, I was very healthy until my 40s when I began to gain weight (and "inflammation" – a puffy, swollen look). This led to high cholesterol, high blood pressure, etc. The medicines they gave me for these conditions caused other issues: fatigue, brain fog, joint pain, irritability. Around the 1990s, with Dr. Atkins, many of these American health problems (obesity, heart disease, cancer diabetes, psychological disorders) began to be linked to diet: especially refined or processed foods (carbs: flour/sugar; oils: trans fats; meats, eggs raised with antibiotics and growth hormones; and chemical flavorings, additives, and preservatives).

Many "Alternative Medicine" sites appeared on the web, such as Dr. Mercola, advising natural diets with fiber (chia), oils (coconut, hemp, sunflower), grass-fed beef and free-range eggs and poultry, and wild-caught salmon.

I probably wouldn't have been affected by these developments in nutrition if it hadn't been for my teeth. Or rather, braces on my teeth. I'd never gotten braces in my teens and a family overbite and spaces led me to get "adult braces" at age 56! The metal braces hurt my mouth for two years, I found myself drawn to soft foods: oatmeal, soup, yogurt, etc. Soon I noticed I was feeling better and losing weight! Now, to give an example, my breakfast consists of an oatmeal mixture of steel cut (Irish) oatmeal, sunflower lecithin, chia seeds, and flax seeds. Added to it are oil (coconut, hemp, and pumpkin seed), butter, various probiotics, spices, longan fruit, protein powder, and maple syrup. Delicious and very satisfying.

Tea (India Assam, rooibos, chai, lemongrass, jasmine, mate and matcha) with raw honey and orange (and dark chocolate) keep me going until lunch and dinner (natural beef, eggs, salmon, herring, cabbage coleslaw, lamb, duck, turkey) cheese, wild rice, popcorn, nuts, and seeds. I don't drink alcohol (except a glass of port on New Year's Eve) and the occasional cigar.

My brother Chuck, an aviation physiologist in the Navy was already knowledgeable in nutrition/fitness. He advised healthy oils (especially coconut), fibers (chia seeds), distilled water, and many supplements like bamboo extract, ubiquinol (CoQ-10), and vitamins B12 (sublingual) for energy; probiotics for the immune system; minerals (magnesium/potassium, etc.), spices (especially India – turmeric, Holy basil). I use many others, including Valerian for sleep; CBD broad spectrum for pain; and plantain and serrapeptase for congestion, and skin exfoliation. I just discovered ISO Thrive, a prebiotic that helps digestion, weight, and immunity.

I also use acupressure, the ancient Chinese system of body "pressure points" for relaxation and well-being. Every day, twice, I lie on the bed, legs elevated by pillows, head in a "neck cradle", and press five spots on the abdomen and chest (especially "The Sea of Tranquility") that cause deep breathing, stress relief, and usually falling asleep! I also alternate days swimming and taking Epsom salt baths. Walking is another favorite. Sunshine for Vitamin D. All of these make me feel very good, flexible, pain-free, and happy. Also, because of still frequent back "injuries," I see a Doctor of Osteopathy, Dr. Dalton, in my town, who adjusts and balances my system for greater relief.

Sadly, I think, much of American illness is due to poor diet, dehydration, stress, and lack of good sleep.

Mental Health

In the early 1990s I was diagnosed with Major Depression caused by very stressful situations in *every* aspect of my life (family, work, church, community, profession, etc.). It manifested itself in my not just being sad, but "hypersomnia" (sleeping all the time), panic attacks, and general exhaustion. Picking up a pencil seemed like an enormous effort.

My doctor immediately diagnosed it and prescribed the anti-depressant drug of the time: Prozac. Within a week I felt better – cheerful, and energized, for the three months I was on it and for four months after I got off it. Then I felt the depression come back due to renewed stress and went back on Prozac for a month. But by then, I had learned to recognize the symptoms of the disorder coming on: like a dark cloud coming over my brain. I learned that when that state came on I must get away from stress to avoid a relapse. Fortunately, my family was understanding, and my jobs (college professor and church minister) had flexible enough schedules that I could "take off" when I felt the stress becoming too much.

I also learned that doing things one likes: walks in the country, music, funny TV (*Rumpole Andy Griffith*) and movies (W. C. Fields Bob Hope), light reading (P. G. Wodehouse, John Mortimer, Peanuts cartoons), and being with friends, combats depression.

The Bible says that "laughter is a medicine" and I have found that true in keeping the depression away these past thirty years.

Stress and the mental illness it causes is a great epidemic of our time. Constant pressure, demands, and interruptions, all increase this stress and the psychological problems it causes.

My experience is that "getting away" from this world of trouble is essential. Even Jesus took off to the mountains to be alone with God. The greatest stress reliever is my Christian Faith and prayer. Contemplation, worship, sacred music, study, and devotion take me away from life's stresses and allow me to be both happy and productive, encouraging others.

SPORTS & ENTERTAINMENT

I never was much involved in team sports (baseball, basketball, football, soccer) but rather in more "individual" sports: tennis, swimming, sailing. I don't know why, but I even find watching team sports boring. Even exciting car races, I find dull, noisy, monotonous. And "school spirit" around sports I never understood. It seemed a misplaced enthusiasm.

Even at my Oxford College, Wycliffe Hall (a theological school!) I once was shocked to walk into the Senior Common (student) Room during a televised soccer game and heard screaming, anger, hatred, and the most extreme tribalism. I know Europeans take soccer very seriously, and perhaps it's a healthy release of tension, but I could never relate to its emotional intensity.

Tennis, swimming, and sailing are more testing "yourself" against a standard. And when I played tennis in the 1960-70's it was a "Gentleman's Game" – calm, polite, non-competitive. It was customary to complement one's opponent on a good shot and mostly just lob the ball gently, not hitting hard or shots hard to return. And, of course, jumping over the net if you won, shaking your opponent's hand, and saying, "Good Game". All are very civilized. Mostly it was to enjoy being outside: the sunshine, fresh air, and exercise.

I once heard a funny joke about tournament psychology. Since our summer tennis tournaments at the CSA and my school teams were not strict about team sports dress, the idea was to find out what your opponent would be wearing: casual or "tennis whites". If he showed up in a casual dress, you would wear whites and say, "Well, if we're going to take the game *seriously*, we *should* dress the part." If he was going to wear whites, you'd show up casually dressed and say, "Well, it doesn't really matter what you wear; it's how you play the game." Psych him out.

The most confusing game I've ever watched was English cricket. The Oxford Cricket Club field was right next to my College and I often watched. Incomprehensible, giving rise to many jokes and even a wall hanging, "The Ins-and-Outs of Cricket" given me by Michael Lloyd and hanging in my loft today.

The best of sports develops, like arts, a team spirit, comradery, and working together. I recall the champion women's lacrosse team at UVA-Wise, many of whose members were some of my best students in Political Theory as well as being gifted athletes. They obviously had a great community and fun as well as hard work and competition. Sadly, many of them were seniors when the COVID-19 virus shut down their season just as they were about to win a major regional championship.

Some kind of physical activity, sport, or recreation should balance passive intellectual or entertainment activity. The old Greek "Mind-Body" balance of a healthy individual.

Musical Entertainment

As I mentioned in the "Health" chapter, it has been my Faith, Friends, and Music that has kept me sane.

My favorite music is Classical, not from any snobbery or sophistication; I just find it beautiful, uplifting, and comforting.

My parents had the 1950s "Hi-Fi" record player in the living room with mostly "33's" of their era – Big Bands, Swing, and Jazz. But among these, I found a few Classical records: Bach, Mozart, and Beethoven (probably from my mother's collection). I was immediately attracted to this 18th-century music and listened to it over and over.

In college, I began collecting Classical music: records, tapes, then discs. My favorite composers were Mozart, Haydn, Vivaldi, Telemann, and Handel. I'd also always liked Medieval Choral (Church) music, but I didn't realize that my favorite Classical composers wrote much religious music – "Sacred" music for church services.

Everyone knew Handel's *Messiah* and Mozart's *Requiem,* but it wasn't until I lived in Vienna, Austria, that I heard (at the Opera House, concerts, and Catholic churches) the vast, enormous *corpus* of Classical Sacred music: sung Masses, Vespers music, funeral Requiems, etc. It became my favorite music. The lively, light, beautiful Classical style with Christian themes (a sung Mass or Holy Communion; the Creeds' doctrine; funeral or baptism or special Saints' Days; Lent; Advent; Christmas). Glorious.

Aristotle said that music came out of and evoked certain feelings and these made me feel exalted, joyful, comforted, and peaceful. Soon I had a house-full (and car-full) of Classical religious music and listened to it daily. It improved my mental health. It was therapy. It keeps me in a spiritual, happy mood.

Of course, growing up in the 60's I enjoyed "Classic Rock" (Beatles, Bee-Gees, Beach Boys, etc.) but once popular music turned "Hard" I found it too loud, ugly, and nasty. Even much "soft" popular music one hears in stores and restaurants I find disturbing: ugly, noisy, nasty: expressing dark or evil human emotions. If it is loud, I literally must put cotton in my ears, or it affects my mood negatively.

I also love classic musicals: *My Fair Lady*, *Music Man*, *Singin' in the Rain*, *Wizard of Oz*, *White Christmas*, *101 Dalmatians*, and Gilbert and Sullivan's *HMS Pinafore*. These, like Classical and Sacred music, are light-hearted, and uplifting.

But my favorite Classical and Sacred music aids in meditation, thought, and writing. It is a big part of my life.

TV – Movies – Theater – Literature

It's hard to believe that when I grew up, we had basically three TV channels (ABC, NBC, CBS). At any time of the day (except between about 11:00 p.m. and 5:00 a.m. when they went "off the air") you could choose one of three programs to watch. No wonder everyone thought the same!

Then in the 1980's, cable TV came in with hundreds of channels. Then video streaming on the internet with thousands of sites. So, my taste in TV entertainment comes out of this limited venue. Now with video tapes and DVD videos, we can collect our favorite shows and watch them when we want.

I favor light comedy shows: *Andy Griffith*; *Leave It to Beaver*; *Bob Newhart*; *Sanford and Son*; *Larry David*; and *The Office*. And British comedies: *Rumpole*; *All Creatures Great and Small*; *The Irish R. M.*; *Benny Hill*; *The I. T. Crowd*; *Brideshead Revisited*; and *Downton Abbey*.

When I grew up, I had to go to a movie theater to see movies. Now, with DVDs, I have most of my favorites (again, comedies):

W.C. Fields; Bob Hope and Bing Crosby; Woody Allen; Cary Grant; and a few serious films: *Amadeus*; *The Emperor's Club*; *Chariots of Fire*; *A Wonderful Life*. I'm afraid I find most contemporary movies boring, vulgar, and politicized.

Live theater has become more a part of my life as family members (Elaine with college and high school productions and P. J. with Shakespeare, etc.) are involved. I find "real" live performances add a dimension to entertainment. The play version of *The Great Gatsby* was the only one I understood (after both reading the book and seeing the movie).

My taste in reading seems to follow TV, movies, and theater: light, funny, comedies. Nineteenth Century English and American writers: Trollope; Hawthorne; Twain; James; Matthew Arnold; Osbert Lancaster; P. G. Wodehouse; Evelyn Waugh; Kingsley Amis; John Mortimer. Some of these last ones are barely 20th Century, Victorian, and Edwardian. It shows my cultural affinity to that era, growing from my Midwest, middle-class background. Like TV and movies, I have difficulty identifying with or enjoying most modern writing.

As I mentioned earlier about music, I believe good art, theater, visual entertainment, especially comedy, to perform a great humanitarian service: to cheer people up in this often-sad world. And I have to admit, with some embarrassment, that the really light reading of my youth (*Hardy Boys* books, "Archie", and "Peanuts" cartoons) is increasingly the comfort of my old age.

I'm not completely frivolous though. I start each day by reading the Bible and for a religious devotional: Oswald Chambers; C. S. Lewis; St. Augustine. Then I move on to slightly less serious literature and "Snoopy" cartoons. . .

CARS

Like most American boys of my era (1950s – 70s), I loved cars, especially sports cars. The style, ride, handling, and dash of a sporty car made getting our driver's licenses (age 16) exciting.

I was blessed, due to a small inheritance, to buy a brand-new British Triumph "Spitfire". Small, low-slung, shapely, it was a perfect two-seater convertible, burgundy with tan leather, sports car for a teen. Despite its small (four-cylinder) engine and typical British unreliability, it was so fun to drive, handled so well, and looked so good. It was so small, that I could barely get in and out of it as a skinny sixteen-year-old. I expect I couldn't get my right foot in it now...

A couple of years later, I sold the Triumph and bought my brother's 1963 Corvette Stingray – equally dashing but enormously powerful and fast.

In college, as a "cool" Liberal intellectual, I bought "the serious academic's car" – a 1967 Volvo 122S Swedish sedan that looked like something out of the 1930s. But very functional and reliable. And dull. But I can't believe it took me cross-country several times, from New Mexico to the Eastern United States.

As I was just finishing up graduate school, I celebrated my Ph.D. with a 1972 Jaguar XJ6 – an enormous (but sporty) sedan. Again, in the classic British colors of burgundy with tan leather upholstery. What a smooth ride but with great power and road-hugging handling. Years later, I traded it for an old International Travel-all – a sort of prehistoric Chevy Suburban or large farm wagon. At that time, I was drawn back to the big American cars of my youth: a 1983 Olds 98, a Cadillac Brougham, and finally another sports car: a 1976 Jaguar XJS. The "Best of Both Worlds": an American luxury sedan (1987 Cadillac Fleetwood Brougham) and the twelve-cylinder (8 miles to the gallon!) Jaguar sports car. The former for smooth, quiet long trips; the latter for zipping around local winding mountain roads. Together, they didn't cost $10,000 to buy. I may have to get a Harley motorcycle for my dotage. All require an experienced local mechanic, whom I have in Randy at Lonesome Pine Tire.

Until recently, American cars were known for their style, variety, and performance. Now, they seem all the same and boring. Three styles seem to dominate the world: a small sedan, a balloon-shaped SUV, and a GIANT pickup truck (resembling a freight train engine). To me, ugly and boring.

Everywhere I go, a crowd gathers around my big American luxury sedan or Jaguar sports car. People (especially young men) love the style and performance of these old cars. Maybe they'll make a comeback from Globalist uniformity and mediocrity. For most of their history, cars were not just for transportation, but for fun.

The big leather seats, wood dashboard, large door handles, enormous size, and weight of the doors on the Cadillac; the sleek lines of the Jag. An old farm woman in a pickup truck looked at the Jag and declared, "Sir, that is SOME car!"

The Caddy

Now, when my college-aged daughter got in the Jaguar for the first time and observed the cracking maple dashboard and aged headliner she said, "Boy, Buster, how old IS this car?!!!" But they're not boring.

ANIMALS

Pets

As I mentioned in the "Childhood" chapter, domestic animals, especially dogs and cats, have been an important part of my life, in giving joy, cheer, comfort, fun, and excitement – along with hard work, annoyance, and heartbreak when they die.

"Sissy", our childhood dachshund provided love, joy, happiness, and fun badly needed in our troubled home. She may literally have made the difference between emotional survival and destruction.

In college, when my brother Chuck and I shared a house, we had a large male, a long-haired, black cat named "Puma". He was fierce and lively. I've never known another creature who regularly got around by jumping in the air and propelling himself across the room by kicking his back legs against the wall. Flying.

In Princeton, living in a married student apartment as a graduate student, a calico kitten appeared at our front door. "Thumbelina" was not only one of the sweetest creatures but her comforting presence on my lap probably got me through the Ph.D. comprehensive exams and doctoral dissertation.

In Virginia, we have had a LARGE variety of pets. Living in the country in Powell Valley, I once said that every stray dog in Wise County ended up on our farm where our children would invariably adopt them. At one point, we had four dogs (outside) and four cats (inside) along with assorted hamsters, mice, rabbits, fish, and birds as kids' pets.

I recall one summer night when a bat flew into the house and we couldn't get it out. I'd sent the children into their rooms. Finally, I called to Gwen, "Let Cuddles (her black Persian cat) out of your room." The cat came strolling out, spotted the bat, leaped onto the back of my recliner chair, and ZIP – out flew the bat.

The dogs were "Socks" (a male Collie-Shepherd); "Brownie" (a female German shepherd); "Blackie" (a female Black Lab); and "Whitey (a Siberian Samoyed). The house cats were similarly varied in size, gender, age, and disposition. Lively.

As the children grew up and went off to university and then to their own homes, the number of animals diminished until we had none "of our own". But, living in the country, there are always neighborhood "critters".

The latest is a large, pure-bred German Shepherd, "Maggie", who "belongs" to our neighbors, the Kennedys. Before her current status in pens and on leads (because of problems with other dogs in the area) she ran free and accompanied me on my walks and sitting on the deck. She displays all the intelligence, loyalty, and fierceness of her breed. And, as such, this "Queen of Guard Dogs" has saved my life on at least two occasions.

The first was one autumn morning walk down my wooded lane when out of the trees an enormous hawk descended on me, talons the size of my hand extended and coming straight for my face. Out of the corner of my eyes, I saw Maggie coming across the bridge about twenty yards away and called to her. She spotted the hawk and raced towards it, diverting it just before it tore my face off, possibly killing me. I had actually raised my arms over my face (a natural reflex impulse) but that would have meant the arteries in my arms torn apart and bleeding to death. Needless to say, I was very grateful to this dog and have rewarded her since with prime scraps of steak, salmon, and turkey.

The other time was when an escaped murderer was loose in the area. The woods around my house would have been a perfect place to hide, and being alone that night, I was anxious. Maggie, as I've heard of other dogs, sensed my anxiety and patrolled the house all night!

Besides Maggie and her sister, "Josie", we have no plans to get other animals at our age. But I am grateful for the companionship, joy, and protection all our pets have provided.

CLOTHES

I grew up with the old adage "The clothes make the man." This meant that one's appearance reflected and reinforced one's character, personality, and reliability. This didn't mean "fancy" or expensive clothes; just adhering to certain standards of taste and decorum.

For most adult men of middle-class, professional status, this meant a dark suit (blue, black, or gray) or at least a sport coat and dress pants worn with a white dress shirt (or powder blue, if you were daring) with a formal or button-down collar; a mid-width tie of subdued color and design (dark blue or burgundy print or diagonal stripes); dark shoes and socks. Unostentatious, this "uniform" was actually to "downplay" one's clothes so that one's facial countenance and manner were emphasized.

By the 1960's this standard of dressing was shaken up and, by the time I retired from the College in 2019, I was the only faculty member who adhered to it.

The key was not to be "flashy" or "tacky" with bright colors, designs, opulence, or lack of coverage.

One of my favorite TV shows, *Bob Newhart*, who played a professional in the Midwest, pained me because by the 1970's he wore suits of cheap fabric (polyester) of bright and odd colors (e.g., light blue) with wide lapels and very wide "loud" ties of abstract patterns. It would be hard to take someone seriously who dressed like that. I admit this is a prejudice. And that sense of order was cast out like most in the 1960's.

Even in casual wear, certain standards existed. Polo shirts with collars, not "T-shirts" (especially not with designs on them!); khaki pants, not blue jeans. Matching colors and designs. It all seems very old-fashioned now. Even in domestic wear standards were upheld. Robes and pajamas. Always dressed for outside when coming downstairs. I don't know why, but when staying at my grandparents at age five, I thought this didn't apply and came down to the breakfast table in pajamas to find everyone else dressed. Sitting next to my grandpa, he just looked at me, smiled, and said, "Comfortable?"

The only justification I can think of for these standards of appearance (including make-up, facial hair, and elaborate hairdos) was the one my military-career brother gave for the many formalities in the Navy. Small details trained discipline for large details, reliability, and standards.

The "anything goes" contemporary culture in clothing reflects a looseness in other manners, morals, and standards.

Culture

It is the same with "culture" – music, art, architecture – as with clothing. The "better" culture determined over the years (Mozart, da Vinci, Gothic, Baroque, etc.) affects and reflects one's quality. What we hear, see, and touch affects our personality, character, and happiness.

I've never understood the appeal of ugly music, murals, and buildings. Beauty "uplifts" our minds and souls; nasty, hard, ugly things hurt our nature and make us bad.

The old phrase "ugly as sin" implies that immorality is ugly (however it disguises itself as chic or fashionable). Goodness and virtue are beautiful, even if plain.

On a deeper level of culture, as the philosopher Edmund Burke shows, our institutions, education, and even the community: food, design, and clothing, affect our human nature. Culture in the Burkean sense includes the best literature, art, philosophy, and music of the past, which civilizes the present and future.

LEADERSHIP AND CON MEN

A leader sets the tone for the entire organization. If the leader is competent, qualified, kind, diligent, and personable, the whole organization will run smoothly and happily. If the leader is incompetent, unqualified, corrupt, difficult, vain, proud, or selfish, those negative qualities will infect the entire organization and it will be ineffective and miserable, contentious, and eventually ruined.

I think leadership is a gift. We can learn effective traits of a leader, but some seem to just naturally lead with grace, confidence, and success. I think of Sheriff Taylor on *The Andy Griffith Show*: intelligent, dedicated, having high professional standards, but flexible, kind, friendly, merciful, setting a tone of security and goodness.

St. Augustine describes good leadership as:

> To rebuke those who stir up strife, comfort those of little courage, take the part of the weak, refute opponents, and guard against traps. They teach the ignorant, awake the indolent, put the presumptuous in their place, mollify the quarrelsome, help the poor, liberate the oppressed, encourage the good, suffer the wicked, and love everyone.

That kind of leader builds up and prospers an organization, making people pleased to be a part of it. We all wish for such a boss, ruler, minister, teacher, commanding officer, judge.

I can't judge, as my three terms (or "sentences" of three years, six years, and ten years) as Department Chair at the College were not the best. My style was probably too *laissez-faire* – "live and let live". I just left people alone, expecting them to be professional, do their jobs, and leave *me* alone, except when they had a legitimate need. My church ministry has been better, I think, partly because of the maturity and dedication of the members.

But I've seen the positive effects of good leadership and the disasters of poor leadership in all the organizations I've known:

academic, religious, corporate, social, foundations, colleges, campus ministry, churches, and clubs.

The first and foremost requirement is what Plato calls the "art" of the organization. If heading a university, to be above all "an academic" – knowing and living the ideals of education. Not primarily political (with causes, agendas, ideologies) or economic (concerned with budgets, fund-raising, marketing). I once remarked to a president, "If we take care of the academic, focus on that, the political and economic will take care of themselves. We will be just and prosperous. But, if we subordinate the "art" purpose of the institution for subordinate concerns, it's like the tail wagging the dog." Nothing will succeed.

I've seen cherished institutions prosperous, effective positive over decades destroyed in a few years under bad leadership. It's heartbreaking, but then, effective leaders can appear (often from unexpected places) and build an organization up quickly. So, there is always hope. But truly great leadership is rare.

CON MEN

Perhaps the opposite of good leadership is corrupt, dishonest "leadership". I don't know if there are *more* con men operating now or if I've just encountered more of them in the past few years. By "con men" I mean people who appear good and effective but who cheat and use people for their wicked and selfish purposes.

They are usually perfectly respectable-looking, usually middle-aged, old men, distinguished, respectable heads of organizations, foundations, schools, and even churches. They may practice the most basic "con" – stealing money for themselves portrayed as supporting good works, service, and ideals. But, more often, I've found, it is a "con" to use others for their own power, prestige, reputation, prosperity, and control.

I'm afraid I've become rather too cautious, and almost cynical when someone, or a group, approaches me for "help", advice, or assistance. We should, especially as Christians, be open to appeals, and opportunities to help. But as Jesus instructed us to be, "shrewd as a serpent and innocent as a dove". To see through the disguised evil, but remain hopeful, pure, and helpful.

Unless there is clear evidence of a con (or a distinct "feeling" – warning from God) we should be welcoming, cooperative, and polite. In the end, we trust in God's protection and guidance. Even when I was "fooled' for a while by a clever con artist, it was usually not for a great amount or with serious damage.

If such con-jobs are in fact on the rise, we should be vigilant without being uncharitable. It's rare in a world of so many scams, tricks, and pitfalls, but that's why we have to stay close to God and His Truth.

RETIREMENT

Most working Americans work for 30-40 years, contributing to Social Security and possibly a company pension plan which provides an income after they stop earning.

I retired from the College at age 65. There was no mandatory retirement age, but the quality and pleasure of higher education had declined so it was easier to retire, especially after having a very rewarding academic career. Many of my colleagues stayed on to age 70 or more as they felt fit and would find retirement boring. I stayed on until 65 because I saw many who continued to lose their mental faculties between 65 and 70. And the last few sad years were what people remembered.

Also, I have found retirement not boring in the least. Writing this *Memoir*, continuing part-time at the church, traveling, keeping in touch with friends, correspondence, continuing research, etc., have kept me well occupied, albeit at a slower, more leisurely pace.

Beginning in my late 50's, I found my energy level going down. So, it is nice to enjoy a reduced workload and spend more time walking, swimming, resting, contemplating, and reminiscing. There are also opportunities to speak or give guest lectures at colleges and universities that still respect academic freedom. And I joined the "Digital Age" by writing short pieces for political blogs, at the encouragement of my friend and colleague, Constitutional Law scholar Stephen Presser, (*American Greatness, GENZ Conservative, etc.*) applying Classical Political Theory, history, and law to contemporary events.

Driving my old cars within a five-mile radius is pleasant, not pressured or hurried.

I've had time to just *read* – not for a lecture, or an article, or a book review, but just for pleasure. Washington Irving, Henry James, Oscar Wilde, Evelyn Waugh. Just for the interest and enjoyment of it.

I regularly have lunch or tea with friends at a good local restaurant or in my loft. The lack of a strict work schedule makes trips and vacations much easier. Freedom. Leisure. No rush. I cannot imagine, after two years of retirement, going back to a "full-time" job with its stress, busy life, and difficulties.

Also, as you get older, you must give more attention to your health – eating, sleeping, and exercising. The main causes of illness in our society are poor diet, stress, and sleep deprivation. As you get older those cause increased health problems. So "taking care of yourself" isn't just to live longer, but to be happy and healthy as you live.

I am enormously grateful that I have been blessed with a peaceful and prosperous but productive old age in retirement.

DEATH AND LEGACY

My Great-grandfather ended his memoir (*Charles M. Sheldon: His Life Story*) with a chapter entitled, "Two Old Friends: Old Age and Death". His description of the benefits of old age is much like mine on "Retirement", but he emphasized "The right to repose": rest, thought, contemplation, after an active and blessed life of activity.

Death is an old friend to the Christian because it is not the end but the beginning of New Life in Heaven – seeing family, friends, and all those who died in the Faith. Never to be separated again. Favorite ones you've never met (C. S. Lewis; Matthew Arnold; Henry James; Aristotle; St. Augustine; Aquinas; Hannah Arendt; Thomas Jefferson; and, of course, our Lord Himself: Jesus).

My "Legacy", I hope, is to leave the world with two things: my Faith and a Laugh. The Truth of God's love through Jesus Christ and the Holy Spirit, and a smile. Something to cheer in this sad, tragic world. One never knows what one will be remembered for. I expect at least as a loving, fun father to my children; and an example of what I see as the most important ideas in Political Theory,

Early American religion and politics, political theology. A recent review of my first book *The History of Political Theory: Ancient Greece to Modern America* (published 33 years ago and used in my year-long survey course for 30 years) by Will Tanner in *GENZ Conservative.com* was just the kind of tribute I'd hoped for: as a book that explains complicated, important ideas clearly to the improvement of the world.

But one never knows and really shouldn't care. I recall hearing once that A. A. Milne, the author of the popular children's book *Winnie the Pooh*, was disappointed that his serious work in writing, theater, and society was overshadowed by this silly children's story (now in book form, movie, TV, and cartoon). But while this may not have been the most "important" of his career's work, it has brought joy and laughter to millions. Probably I'll be remembered by my students for my silly jokes and puns. ("Locke is the key to American political thought.") It doesn't matter. We do what the Lord leads us to do and leave the consequences to Him.

One thing I've often looked for in autobiographies (and seldom found) was just the daily life of the person. The ordinary routine would be fascinating to future generations whose lifestyles will invariably be very different. Thomas Jefferson probably provided the greatest insight into his daily life through his letters and family reminiscences. I recall being surprised that in the winter, in the mansion Monticello high on a hill in 18th Century Charlottesville, Virginia (with only fireplaces for heat) he often had to thaw out his frozen ink bottle before he could write!

So, my ordinary life is here.

A Day in the Life. . .

My daily routine as an adult was largely unchanged during a 40-year academic career and now in retirement.

I generally get up early, 4:00-6:00 a.m., and have my oatmeal breakfast (see "Health" chapter) and a pot of tea with raw honey and orange slices. Then I "work" in a large recliner and lap table, (after Bible and/or devotional reading) reading, writing, and thinking.

During my academic career, it was reading and writing for lectures, articles, book chapters, reviews, conference papers, recommendations, and communications.

It may come as a shock to anyone born after 2000, but until my middle age (40s) there was no internet, computers, smartphones, online searches, shopping, email, Facebook, etc. Most communication was by landline telephones and paper mail. Or personal face-to-face conversations with people in the same room!

I recall a history professor coming back to the college after he'd retired in the mid-1990s. Where his department colleagues used to congregate in each other's offices, talk, laugh, and advise students, now, he said, he found each faculty member alone, in his office staring at a screen.

Once I received my Endowed Professorship with a reduced teaching load (two classes per semester), I would schedule classes from late morning through afternoon with office hours, committee meetings, etc. worked in. I generally went in three days a week (Monday, Tuesday, and Thursday). That was considered a luxury when most faculty taught four classes a semester and went in five days a week.

Now, with remote/distance learning, many might consider my onsite schedule heavy! My drive to campus was about 16 miles on a rural four-lane highway and took about 30 minutes with only two stoplights on the way.

I generally have a meal and walk around the land in the late morning. Then a swim or another walk during the late afternoon and tea with snacks (dark chocolate, food bars, toast with orange marmalade or preserves – cherry blackberry, etc.). I may or may not have a light dinner (lunch, meat, fish, rice, yogurt, salad, coleslaw).

I generally watch TV and movies (see "Entertainment" chapter) and possibly make some phone calls/texts/emails/Facebook chats. With all its problematic features, the Digital Age has the advantage of instant communication around the world, especially with family and friends.

Unlike people who grew up with "the web" I often get off my computer and phone, finding they interrupt my peace, solitude, and concentration.

Since retiring, I have spent more time at home with occasional sojourns to swim, go to church or a restaurant, and doctor's appointments. Still being a church pastor, I have routine work (office and class on Wednesday; writing sermons on Friday morning; worship service on Sunday morning; and often unscheduled ministry: hospital visits, funerals, weddings, counseling, etc.).

I have been blessed to have considerable freedom in my work and I find I am more productive and happier when able to follow my own schedule. One advantage of the new remote schooling, work, and relationships may be increased freedom and flexibility in life, though it may mean that people will just work all the time, never having leisure or privacy.

But, as I am about to write in the new "Epilogue" to the revised version of my textbook, *The History of Political Theory*, "The (Possible) Future Political Theory", regardless of the changes in technology and life, the Human Nature of reasoned, social, moral humanity will come out in some form.

My beautiful Southwest Virginia.

AFTERWORD

Henry James summarized my feelings about this *Memoir* in his own autobiography:

> To knock at the door of the past was in a word to see it open to me quite wide – to see the world within begin to "compose" with a grace of its own round the primary figure, see its people itself vividly and insistently.

I have encouraged all my acquaintances to write a memoir or at least record life's events in a diary or a journal, tape, or video form. There is just something about describing it that makes the past more detailed and understandable. That puts the present into perspective and makes it more realistic.

As those 19th Century German philosophers put it: to make the "subjective" also "objective". And to see God's hand in your life.

And, as I'm facing memory loss in old age, as my son P. J. quipped, "Memoirs are a memory gain."

I am grateful to the many who assisted me in this endeavor, especially my assistant and manuscript-preparer, Sandy Jessee!

Printed in the USA
CPSIA information can be obtained
at www.ICGtesting.com
CBHW030607170524
8700CB00003B/204

9 780996 689069